UNLEASHED

**DOMINATE YOUR LIMITATIONS, BREAK THROUGH YOUR BARRIERS,
LIVE AN EXTRAORDINARY LIFE!**

JEROME WADE

UNLEASHED:
Dominate Your Limitations, Break Through Your Barriers,
Live an Extraordinary Life!

© 2016 by Jerome Wade

ISBN-13: 978-0-9984287-0-3

Edited by Jodi Wade, Kim Herrera, and Lloyd Hildebrand
Cover Design by Jesus Cordero, AnointingProductions.com
Interior Layout and Design by James Woosley, FreeAgentPress.com

To the three people who have made my life epic:

My wife, Jodi;
my daughter, Lauren;
and my son, Austin.

You are unleashers of greatness!

CONTENTS

THE STRUGGLE

I SAT AT MY DESK in utter despair. I was beyond frustrated and disheartened. "Why can't I get past this? What is it that is keeping me from moving things forward? Why can't I win again? What's going on? What's wrong with me?" It had been a couple of years since I was on the winning side of things and the battle for success was wearing me thin.

More times than I can count I did everything I knew to marshal the available resources within me to find solutions and to figure things out, but to no avail. I was stuck in a rut of failed attempts, digging myself deeper into a pit of what felt like perpetual defeat. It seemed that I was in a scene from the movie *Groundhog Day* and my failures were on continual replay. It was insanity at its core, and I felt clueless to find the solutions I needed to move forward.

For twenty years leading up to this season of my life, for the most part, it seemed I could do nothing but succeed. I knew the thrill of winning. I successfully launched and led two non–profit organizations as well as a for-profit design-and-build construction business. I once had possessed "the Midas touch," but now I had lost it.

YOU CAN DOMINATE YOUR LIMITATIONS, BREAK THROUGH YOUR BARRIERS, AND LIVE AN EXTRAORDINARY, GREAT LIFE.

I had known the thrill of leading from advantage where everything is in your favor and it just seemed that lady luck had laid the chips out for me. It wasn't effortless but it came naturally. When you have the advantage, it's like magic, and miraculous things do happen. Having the advantage is a game changer.

Somewhere, somehow, I lost the advantage and like a blind man trying to find his way home in an unfamiliar place, I was lost. There seemed to be an invisible force field that would constantly surround itself around every step I would make and move I would try to take. I bruised my head and nose up against that invisible force field more times than I can even count. Something was holding me back, keeping me down and chaining me to frustration and failure.

The one redeeming quality through all of it is that I refused to give up. There were a few times when I was ready to walk away from it all, but I stubbornly and tenaciously stayed in the fight for success, and I'm glad I did.

I can't say for sure if it was my one hundredth time or the one thousandth attempt when I found my breakthrough, but it finally came. It did not reveal itself in an instant but rather through a series of unusual occurrences of self-revelations. It was a journey for sure, not a destination, a journey that I still continue today in my pursuit of an extraordinary life.

I became a student of my limitations. That's how I came to understand the invisible force field that held me at bay. I began to drill down on the root causes of these leashes and am still learning what creates them, but more importantly I'm learning how to overcome them in my pursuit of success.

In all reality, limitations are drawn like magnets to those who are choosing to do something great with their life and professional pursuits. They have always been there and will always be present, but that doesn't mean we have to submit and surrender our dreams to them.

In the pages of this book I am going to name some very clear and present barriers that you will be able to identify in your own pursuit of success. Identifying them is possibly the most difficult part of the struggle. We must recognize them and then develop the discipline to never let them hold us prisoner again.

YOUR COMMITMENT WILL DETERMINE YOUR SUCCESS.

I am committed to doing everything I can to help you get from where you are now to where you want and deserve to be. My goal is to reveal the key principles so that you can dominate your limitations and unleash greater success, impact, and fullness of life. My goal is to accelerate your story forward so that you don't have to face years of frustration, trapped by the invisible force field of barriers that keep all too many from success. My goal is to activate your leadership greatness, accelerate your professional opportunities, and to maximize your personal journey of success.

There's something that is going to be required of you to get there. It is one word that is the hinge-pin of success. If you take it seriously, you will discover that this one word will be the game-changing catalyst that will help you create what you want: COMMITMENT. Keep this on the screen saver of your brain and never let it fade from your thoughts: your commitment will determine your success.

I need you to be fully committed to each chapter in this book, not to just reading them but to personalizing them, applying them, and most importantly living them. The insights in each chapter can and will change your life if you are committed to what each chapter reveals and what each chapter requires.

YOUR INTENSITY WILL DETERMINE YOUR SPEED OF SUCCESS.

Commitment is not the only thing required to move you to new heights of impact and success. There is another powerful word that will change the game for you: INTENSITY. When you couple commitment with intensity, you will begin to see your story change from disadvantage and struggle to energized and activated greatness where you break through your barriers and limitations and achieve your dreams.

Intensity is about marshaling every ounce of your emotional, physical, and mental energy and laser-focusing it to dominate the invisible force field limiting your pursuit of success. What intensity also means is that you are going all out, giving your very best to live and lead from advantage. Where commitment determines your success, your intensity determines the speed of your success.

Your success will be found by befriending commitment and intensity as they will lead you in your journey of dominating your limitations and unleashing your greatness. If you are ready to be UNLEASHED, turn the page and let the journey begin.

THE HAMMER

IT ISN'T UNTIL YOU'RE walking down the main corridor of the Gallerie dell'Accademia in Florence, Italy that you understand the magnitude of what stands before you. At the end of the hall you see him, towering seventeen feet tall, sculpted from marble and finely crafted by the hand of Michelangelo.

Painted and photographed images cannot convey the greatness of this statue. It is only when you are at an arm's length from it that you can truly grasp the majesty of this masterpiece. Standing at the feet of the statue of David is spellbinding. For a moment you get lost in its grandeur, its profound presence, its refined beauty, its shear greatness.

The work involved in a masterpiece of this magnitude is hard to comprehend. How did Michelangelo take such an enormous slab of marble to uncover the greatness within? How did he know where to place each tip of the chisel? How did he know the precise force to use as he released the energy of the hammer? How was he able to stay so focused on such meticulous and protracted work to create his David?

Michelangelo unleashed greatness on the world by fully leveraging everything he was, within and without, and then transferring that into his work. David was only one of Michelangelo's masterpieces. There are many works of art that were created by his hands, each one demonstrating what one person can do when they unleash greatness on the world.

As you pass through the doors of the Gallerie dell'Accademia and enter the main hall where David stands, you first pass several unfinished sculptures. Each of these have their own story, but none of them is complete. They have been called "Michelangelo's

Prisoners." They are unfinished, incomplete, rough and raw works, imprisoned in an unfinished state. Although still far from completed, in their own right, they are still masterpieces.

My favorite "prisoner" is the one they call Atlas. In him you see strength, you see resolve, you see greatness waiting to be unleashed. What you also see in each of them, in a very real way, is the state of their confinement. They are held captive in stone. They are bound to only reflect a part of their true majesty and never to be fully realized. They stand in a perpetual state of waiting to be revealed and unleashed from their prison. Each one of them was intended to be as masterfully done as David. Each one of them was created to be a fine piece of art on display for the world. Each one of them was meant to be a completed work of art.

As I stood in the main hall, I couldn't help but see myself in the "prisoners." David was just a few meters away, standing majestically, towering in a glorious display of greatness. Each of the "prisoners" stood in the shadows of what could be. Each "prisoner" only reflected a small degree of his potential, bound to the disappointment of what could have been.

I found myself identifying with the "prisoners" much more than I could with David. David was the goal, the dream—the state of being fully present, fully aware, and fully complete. He was the model of unleashed greatness. The "prisoners," on the other hand, represent the vast majority of people today: good people who are bound and imprisoned by self-imposed limitations and waiting for the day when someone will take a hammer to chisel and complete the work.

TAKE THE CHISEL AND HAMMER AND DO THE WORK OF CREATING A MASTERPIECE OF LIFE.

You may find yourself identifying with the "prisoners" as well. You too are a rough, raw, and incomplete work of art that is waiting to be great but not knowing how to get there. You are wanting to live fully and make your life count. You want to achieve the success you believe you were meant for, and you want to realize your potential but do not know how to break out of the stone cage that holds you. You too find yourself in suspended animation somewhere between the unfinished "prisoner" and the masterpiece David.

If this is you, you're not alone. In fact, you stand in a very long line of people who know they were meant for more. If this is you, I've got great news: you can still unleash your greatness on the world. You are about to break free from the stone prison that has kept you at a distance from greatness.

Here is the important difference from the stone "prisoners" and you: they will only be released if someone finishes what the sculptor began. For the "prisoners" to be released someone must hold a chisel in their hand and put force to the hammer, whittling away everything that is keeping them from greatness. They are dependent on someone else's work. You, on the other hand, cannot wait for someone else to take a hammer and chisel in hand and get to work. You must muster the courage to hold the chisel and then swing the hammer. You are only a "prisoner" because you have chosen to be one. Your greatness is in your hands, so unleash yourself on the world.

YOUR GREATNESS IS IN YOUR HANDS, SO UNLEASH YOURSELF ON THE WORLD.

I have had a front row seat to witness the release of many "prisoners," as I have helped people find the tools and courage to change the entire course of their lives. It is possible. I have seen many put chisel and hammer in their hands and begin to do the hard work of unleashing their greatness. There are a few key practices that I have discovered that will empower you to turn from your disadvantages and empower you to be unleashed. All of these practices are dependent on you taking the hammer and chisel in hand and committing to do the hard work.

For you to unleash your greatness on the world, more will be required of you than you have ever known. You have what it takes, you have the goods to become the person you were meant to become, but you must want it and want it with resolve.

Let's take inventory and think through where you find yourself right now. There will be a few of you who have found the inner strength and wherewithal to pick up the chisel and hammer, and you have been working diligently to free yourself from your limitations. It is a glorious day when you own the task and do the work of setting yourself free.

YOU HAVE WHAT IT TAKES TO LIVE AN EXTRAORDINARILY GREAT LIFE.

There are many others, quite probably most of you reading this, who are trapped in your own marble slab encasement, wanting things to be different but exhausted or despairing from trying to figure a way to a bigger, brighter, and better future, but to no avail.

The very first step is to identify what it is that holds you prisoner. When I say you must identify it, I am not saying that you simply acknowledge that you are trapped by limitations; you must get specific, call it out, give it a name or a label and be crystal clear about what it is. When you don't know who your enemy is, you can't fight an intelligent battle to defeat it.

WHEN YOU DON'T SPECIFICALLY KNOW WHAT YOUR LIMITATIONS ARE, YOU CAN'T FIGHT AN INTELLIGENT BATTLE TO DOMINATE THEM.

My marble prison was fear. Those who know me personally know me as a fearless man who seeks out adventure and who often takes risks that seem unreasonable and maybe sometimes irrational. For me to identify my biggest limitation as fear doesn't compute for the person and leader that I project on the outside, but the truth is that I became a prisoner of fear after achieving epic success. It was a fear that I had never known before, but it took hold of me and held fast, nearly derailing everything I loved.

I feared losing the success that I had achieved. I stopped forging an aggressive track forward and became consumed with worry and doubt. I would awake in the middle of the night trapped by overwhelming and paralyzing fear that I didn't have what it took to sustain and grow our success. I allowed poor performance and disruptive behavior from people that I should have dealt with but I was a coward. A few months turned into a few years and it knocked the wind out of me. It wasn't until I wanted out of this fear-filled prison that I got serious about taking the hammer and chisel and doing the work of freeing myself from my self-imposed, marble-encased limitations.

DON'T LET SHAME AND BLAME KEEP YOU FROM THE CHANGE THAT MUST TAKE PLACE.

The first step that created a new momentum for me was to identify what was holding me back and specifically call it out. I was ashamed of myself at first and embarrassed that I had let so many years pass, consumed by my pervasive fear.

There is no win in playing the shame-and-blame game, so I refused to let that become a new prison for me. Work had to be done. I had to place the chisel properly and then swing the hammer.

Fear was not my only prison; I had a few others, so I did the chisel-and-hammer work on each of them and I have learned to dominate them. They no longer own me, I own them.

What is your monolithic marble prison? Like Michelangelo's "prisoners," how are you trapped in your own marble confinement? Get specific. Name it/them, call it/them out. Own it/them. Confront it/them. Don't go to the next chapter without taking this first step. Your extraordinary life is on the other side of identifying your limitations. Before you can dominate, you must identify.

HAVE THE COURAGE TO BE HONEST ABOUT YOUR STRUGGLE AND THEN HAVE THE BRASS TO PICK UP THE HAMMER AND CHISEL AND SET YOURSELF FREE.

If you are struggling to understand your limitations, find a couple of trusted friends, co-workers, your spouse, or boss and ask them to help you see what you cannot see. Have the courage to be honest about your struggle and then have the brass to pick up the hammer and chisel and set yourself free. You have the power within to create the life you want and deserve, so don't settle for anything less. The world needs you to unleash your greatness.

Let's get real by answering a few key questions:

1. What specifically is keeping you from the success you want?

_____

_____

_____

_____

_____

_____

2. What precisely is limiting you?

_____

_____

_____

_____

_____

_____

3. What's the name(s) of your "marble prison"?

_____

_____

_____

_____

_____

4. What is the one thing that if you eliminated it would change the game for you and fuel greater achievement?

_____

_____

_____

_____

_____

_____

THE ADVANTAGE

I T WAS A LATE summer day, September 11, 1297, when William Wallace was about to engage in the first battle for Scottish independence. The Scots were facing insurmountable odds. Reportedly Wallace and his men were outnumbered 10 to 1 with 10,000 English to 1,000 Scots.

Most men might let the odds defeat them before they step on the battlefield, but not Wallace. Retreating in defeat was unconscionable, not even a remote possibility. He was fighting for his countrymen, and they were fighting for their freedom, engaged in a fierce struggle to end the tyranny of the English. For centuries, the Scots had been under the tyranny and domination of the English. They had only known oppression and dreamed of a day when they would be free.

Fueled by his mission to free the Scots and refusing to be deterred, Wallace chose to strategically advance his efforts by leading with a mastery of strategic brilliance. William marshaled uncommon battlefield intelligence. Like a seasoned general, he rejected his disadvantage and used the odds to his advantage. He chose to break free of the lids of oppression and the leashes of the English lords. He was done with the limitations forced upon them, the Scots deserved to be free and Wallace would lead them to it.

YOU CAN GAIN THE ADVANTAGE TO BREAK FREE FROM THE LIDS OTHERS HAVE PLACED ON YOU.

The ensuing battle would take place in Stirling, Scotland. Knowing the lay of the land, Wallace positioned his men near the Stirling Bridge where the English would have to cross to engage in battle. The Stirling Bridge was narrow, at best two horses wide, and it was of some length as it crossed the width of the River Forth.

Wallace would use this bridge to create a choke point to take advantage of the English. A choke point is when you have positioned yourself in a place of strategic advantage and your enemy at a place of strategic disadvantage.

In this case the Scots forced the English to cross the Stirling Bridge and used the bridge to give them the advantage they needed to defeat an army that was ten times their size. It is possible that the English closed their eyes to the obvious choke point or that they were blinded by hubris. In either case, Wallace gained the advantage and overcame his opponent.

The Scots displayed uncommon discipline in waiting for the exact moment to fully maximize the advantage they had created. Archers, swordsmen, and spearmen were strategically placed and standing ready for the order to attack. Wallace waited like a lion, anticipating the exact moment to pounce on his prey.

If he issued the order too soon, their efforts would have been wasted. If he issued the order too late, they could have been overwhelmed and ultimately defeated. With precision and discipline Wallace held his men until more than 5500 English had crossed the bridge, and then he unleashed fury. Wallace released the greatness of his warriors, and they pounded the English with savage, brute force.

NEVER LET THE ODDS DEFEAT YOU BEFORE YOU HAVE ENGAGED IN THE BATTLE FOR YOUR SUCCESS.

The English were caught in their place of disadvantage, caught in the choke point just as Wallace had planned. With the Scots advancing and arrows and spears flying, the English had nowhere to go. They were backed into a corner by their own doing. They were trapped between the advancing Scots and the River Forth. The River Forth was too deep to cross on foot; most of the soldiers wore heavy body armor and those who tried to swim drowned. The Stirling Bridge was packed with man and beast and locked down like a vault.

Wallace took full advantage of the choke point and slaughtered the English. It was a devastating blow, a battle the English should have won hands down, but they lost because of their own arrogance or ignorance or both. Wallace gained the advantage by marshaling intelligent leadership and leveraging a choke point, and it changed the game. Wallace was not the only one to understand the power of gaining the advantage. The greatest success stories of history detail how someone overcame their disadvantage(s), gained the advantage and changed the world. When you have the advantage you have the upper hand and you win.

WHEN YOU MARSHAL INTELLIGENT SELF-LEADERSHIP YOU CAN DEFEAT ANY LIMITATION THAT IS HOLDING YOU BACK.

Let's take a moment to consider two specific areas of life where choke points create a very low ceiling that diminishes and minimizes our lives. The first category that needs our attention is our personal choke points.

Personal choke points are those limiters that can be very hard to detect and often fly under the radar for years. A personal choke point is a behavior or practice that is often ignored as it continues to become an increasing problem. Personal choke points can be attitudes, beliefs, habits, poor behaviors, unhealthy relationships, bad decisions, and the list continues. There's no way for me to write a comprehensive list. Suffice it to say that personal choke points are limiters that affect everything we do personally and interpersonally. They must be identified and eliminated in order for us to achieve our true potential.

BE COURAGEOUS AS YOU IDENTIFY YOUR PERSONAL AND PROFESSIONAL CHOKE POINTS.

The second area of our lives in which choke points create disadvantages is in our professional lives. I have met numerous people who wanted more and greater success, but it seemed like they kept beating their head against the ceiling. They get to a place of defeated frustration and then resignation as they accept that greatness is not their lot in life. Professional choke points are performance limiters that affect the overall trajectory of our career.

These surface in many forms, but most commonly surface as a lack of focus, discipline, or commitment, a lack of experience or the right education, ego, and the list goes on. Moving your professional life forward requires a sober assessment of what is not working and recognizing the painful reality of why. Those who have the courage to confront their professional choke points head on are the ones who unleash their greatness on the world.

Let's take a few minutes now to carefully evaluate what personal and professional choke points may be limiting your potential. Ask the following questions (this is not an easy exercise but it is essential to your success pursuits):

1. What choke points do I need to own that are specifically keeping me from the life I want?

As you answer this first question, leave no stone unturned. This may create some discomfort and even personal pain as you allow possible choke points to surface, but go ahead and lean into the discomfort and pain. Your success is on the other side of eliminating the choke points. The pain and discomfort are only temporary; they fade as you begin to eliminate the choke points in your life and experience immediate results.

_____

_____

_____

_____

_____

_____

_____

2. What changes do I need to make personally to live the life that I dream?

In the introduction I asked you for your absolute commitment to not only reading each chapter but to personalizing and processing each insight and then acting on them. Your commitment to your success will be proven and tested by the courage and resolve you put forth to make the necessary changes. To get from where you are now to where you want to be, you will have to embrace discomfort and pain, but it will be worth it. The life you dream about will only come as you stay committed to the changes that will lead you to success.

_____

_____

_____

_____

_____

_____

_____

3. What choke points are standing in the way of my professional dreams and ambitions?

As you think about your professional pursuits, begin to identify anything that may be holding you back from the professional success you dream of. Don't allow the shame or pride that may likely surface keep you from discovering what you must do to achieve greater success. Be careful to not allow yourself to blame circumstances or situations or people for where you are or where you are not. You must own your success, every part of it.

_____

_____

_____

_____

_____

_____

_____

_____

_____

_____

4. What have I been refusing to hear from other people that can help me identify my choke points?

This question can be complicated. It's difficult enough to hear people we love and trust give us constructive criticism, but when our enemies provide their uninvited input and opinion, it's a completely different thing. Let me encourage you to not dismiss even the criticism of your enemies. Even from the lips of your worst enemy, there may be a grain of truth that could change the game for you. Let their wisdom, not their poison, speak to you. If they have given you a hard truth that you needed to hear, they have given you a gift.

----

5. How am I going to make sure that I follow through with what I have processed in the questions above?

How you implement the insights within this book is the ultimate goal. It is why I wrote this book and why you are holding it in your hands. You can waste the gift I am giving you and the time you have spent to read this book, or you can fully leverage it to your advantage. As you do the hard work of identifying and dominating your limitations, you create a success process that will ensure long-term results. The best way for this to happen is for you to write down a clear and detailed plan of attack, set real expectations with completion and execution dates and find someone or a group of people who will help you stay focused and hold you to the promises you will make to yourself and to your accountability group.

THE NEW

I T'S A CRISP JANUARY 1st morning; the temperature is somewhere in the neighborhood of four degrees (Fahrenheit). Just outside the window I am looking at the snow-covered peaks that hover above Pagosa Springs, CO. It is a beautiful first day of the year. I know that I am not alone in how I feel about the first of the year, but I LOVE IT!

I have always been a raving fan of the new beginning that a new year provides. In many ways it feels like a clean sheet of paper on which to write a greater story for my life. It is an empty canvas that waits for me to take a brush and color it, thereby beginning to paint my own masterpiece. A new year is the dawn of a new adventure with many opportunities and challenges awaiting my first steps. I love new beginnings, don't you?

I spent some time during the last few days reflecting on the previous year. Without going into the details of it, it was a profoundly amazing year for my family and me. We took bold new steps in the pursuit of new dreams and transitioned from a career that we loved to a new one that we love even more. It is truly amazing what can happen in one year's time. In my reflections regarding this past year I found myself grateful; grateful for the favor and rapid development of our new pursuits, for old and new friends, for the life I have lived. I even found myself grateful for the inglorious parts of my journey.

When I say inglorious, I am talking about the parts of my story and experiences that are less than glamorous, less than successful, less than stellar, less than what I would have wanted them to be. Like you, my story has pages that are filled with failed attempts, pain, struggle, and disappointments. As much as I want my story to be one long string of successes, it's not. It is much more a synthesis of both success and failure. What I find most difficult to deal with are my inglorious moments of failed attempts, bad moves, and poor performance. I know that I am in a long line of people who if they were honest would say the same, but fumbling the ball is very difficult for me to process.

EVERYONE HAS A CHAPTER OR TWO IN THEIR BOOK THAT THEY DON'T WANT ANYONE TO READ.

My personality profile shows that I am someone who likes to win and who typically wins big, so any losses are completely devastating to me. When I misstep, or fumble a decision, or react poorly, or blow it, it leaves me feeling wrecked.

In all fairness, I am glad that I am at a place in my life where I am aware of and acknowledge the "not so pretty" realities of my life. However, I often take them too far and hold on to them for too long until they become paralyzing memories that I replay in my mind over and over and over again. I can lament and agonize over my own failures to such a degree that it affects my productivity and performance in every arena of my life, and I spiral into self-loathing.

The solution I have discovered and that I make every effort to live by is found in six words: let it go, and move on. These words have far greater power than we can imagine if we will embrace them and live by them.

SIX OF THE MOST POWERFUL WORDS THAT WILL FUEL YOUR SUCCESS: "LET IT GO, AND MOVE ON."

I recently met with a high-profile executive who has led his business with great success. He has a very disciplined leadership practice and is fully leveraging every opportunity of the market they serve. While everything on the surface is progressing quite well, he struggles with some unresolved parts of his life story.

He was holding on to some things that he just needed to let go of and move on. What he held onto wasn't ever going to be fixed or resolved or restored, for that matter. Instead of perpetuating the problem through repeated regret, there are some things that can only be resolved when we decide to just let it go and intentionally move on.

I coach a number of people who struggle with the same issue: we (including me) keep holding on in hopes of turning a failure into a success, or turning a defeat into a victory, or fixing what is broken. We spend exhausting amounts of time and energy trying to get it right or to make it right when there are some things that you can't fix. Sometimes it's irreparable because it involves other people who don't care to cooperate. Other times the proverbial milk just cannot be put back into the bottle. In any case, we must learn to recognize when it's time to "let it go, and move on." If it can be fixed or righted, then by all means make every effort to do so. But when it becomes obvious that the effort is futile or unproductive, and it is simply perpetuating unnecessary pain and problems, do what needs to be done and let it go; move on.

THERE ARE SOME THINGS THAT WILL NEVER BE MADE RIGHT, SO GIVE YOURSELF PERMISSION TO MOVE ON.

As I launch this new year, the sun is shining and glistening on the snow. I have an empty canvas inviting me to paint a masterpiece, but to do so I have to let a few things go and move on. There are some things that I cannot fix, I cannot repair, I cannot redo, I cannot undo, I cannot make right, despite focused effort and intent. So I say to the inglorious parts of my journey, "Thank you for teaching me, molding me, and shaping me; but today, the first day of this new year (or whatever the date is when you are reading this), I am letting go and moving on."

I am letting go of regret, self-loathing, shame, and blame so that I can embrace what is yet to come. The future is bright, just like the sun is shining and the snow is glistening outside of my window. I will not let the inglorious parts of my past nor the opinions of others hold me prisoner. I am liberating myself from what I cannot change to live a life of unleashed greatness. And I encourage you to do the same.

LIBERATE YOURSELF FROM WHAT YOU CANNOT CHANGE SO THAT YOU CAN LIVE A LIFE OF UNLEASHED GREATNESS.

The reality for all of us is that there are chapters in the book of our life that we don't want anyone to read. They are filled with stories of bloopers and blunders, pain and problems. They are embarrassing and contain content and information that we don't want others to know or believe about us. The point of this chapter is not to surface or resurface the inglorious parts of our story, but to encourage you to do three essential things to embrace the new realities of your life.

The first step in embracing the New You is to accept the past for what it is; the past is the past. It is what it is. What's done is done. This was a hard truth for me to embrace for myself. I wanted to keep nursing my mistakes or the injustices of life and others. I wanted to keep picking at the sore spots of leadership missteps. In so doing, I was perpetuating my pain and problems. In all honesty, what's the point in holding on to the past? What good comes from reliving and reviving the inglorious realities of our story? Nothing good comes from self-loathing and self-condemnation, NOTHING! The sooner you embrace the past for what it is, the happier, more productive, more joyful, and better you will be. So you've made a few mistakes and had a few unfortunate happenings. Simply recognize them for what they are. The past is the past, so embrace the new day so that the New You can surface and your new life can begin.

NOTHING GOOD COMES FROM RELIVING AND REVIVING THE INGLORIOUS PARTS OF YOUR STORY.

The second step in embracing the New You is to see the beauty in your ashes and pain. Even from the most horrific failures and darkest pain we can find an underlying gift. The gift is the person we become as we lead forward from the failed parts of our story. Life has a way of molding and shaping us, and we can choose to be shaped for the good. It is easy to play the victim or to become bitter or to play the blame game. If that is where you are, set yourself free and see the gift in your past so that you fully live in the present and create an extraordinary future.

THERE IS PROFOUND BEAUTY IN YOUR ASHES AND PAIN WHEN YOU SEE THAT WHAT YOU HAVE BEEN THROUGH IN LIFE HAS BEEN A GIFT.

Recently I heard Tony Robbins speaking at one of his Unleash the Power Within seminars. He made a statement that had a profound and liberating effect on my life. He said, "Nothing happens *to* you; it happens *for* you." When he made that statement something resonated deep within me. There was wisdom behind his words that I needed to hear to help me embrace the new. I replayed the entire story of my life, even the shameful parts of my story, and everything changed, instantly. "Nothing happens *to* you; it happens *for* you." In an instant the story of my success and failures reconciled. The self-loathing and regret left me, and I felt the weight I had been carrying lift from my shoulders. I was liberated.

I know that your story might be filled with a few things that are hard for you to reconcile. Maybe it was some evil done to you as a child or as an adult. Maybe it is the greatest failure of your life and you cannot see any good coming from it. I do not want to minimize your pain or your journey, but I do want you to change the way you see it: "This did not happen *to* me, it happened *for* me." I am a better person now. I am a better leader now. I am a new person now. There are too many people who hold on to what happened to them, and they live the entirety of their lives bitter and mad at the world. They live so far beneath the greatness their life was meant to display. Don't let this be your story. Embrace the perspective that nothing happens *to* you, it happens *for* you.

LIVING AN EXTRAORDINARILY GREAT LIFE IS NOT ABOUT EVENTS AND DESTINATIONS BUT ABOUT THE JOURNEY OF BECOMING THE BEST YOU THAT YOU CAN BE.

The third and final step is to enjoy your journey to success. The reality is that success is not a destination; it is a journey. Throughout the journey you will experience the thrill of victory and the agony of defeat. The journey has so much beauty even in our pain if we will only gain the right perspective. Joy and contentment are conscientious choices that must be made daily. You can find joy and purpose even in the darkest hours when you set your mind to embrace the New You.

A close friend of mine was about to celebrate a huge milestone of success when he fumbled the ball and experienced a devastating failure. His choices would leave him at a place of despair and defeat the depths of which he had never experienced before. By all accounts leading up to this moment, he was excelling, advancing, growing, WINNING! And then he lost it all—game over.

I still have vivid memories of the first conversation we had following his derailment. He struggled to make sense of his decisions, including the rhyme and the reason. His thoughts scrambled to make sense of it, but it just didn't add up. He had questions of why, and then how, and then why and how again. What had taken place couldn't be undone. There was no delete button and this wasn't a golf game with his buddies where he would get a mulligan. It was a devastating personal failure. To add insult to injury, it adversely affected his wife and kids and a lot of people who trusted him.

We had several conversations through the years that followed and what should have been a fading past misstep was still very much haunting him in his present. He was unable to let it go and to stop the destructive influences of shame and regret. He was haunted by what couldn't be undone and how it had hurt so many people. Every time we spoke he would bring his past into his present and badger himself with judgment and self-defeating statements. The rest of the world moved on, but he couldn't, for he was prisoner to his past.

SOME FAILURES FEEL FATAL, BUT NONE OF THEM ARE FINAL.

Not only have I walked with many of my personal friends and acquaintances through their own devastations, I too have had to walk through my own personal and professional failures. Some failures feel fatal, but no failure is final unless we allow it to be. Some fail in profound ways with an impressive magnitude of consequence, while others fail in smaller degrees with minor collateral damage. Regardless of the scale, failure is part of living. Failure is as normal to living as breathing is. In fact, failure is the pathway to greatness.

What is constant for every one of us is that failure is normal, and we must learn how to embrace it for what it is: the Sage of Greatness. In EVERY mistake, there are lessons to be learned. In EVERY miscalculation, there are insights to be downloaded. In EVERY dumb decision there are smart truths waiting for us to hear what they have to say. In EVERY botched attempt, knowledge knocks on the door to educate us. In EVERY failure, wisdom whispers to inform us of the way to greatness.

FAILURE IS AS NORMAL AS BREATHING AND IS ESSENTIAL TO YOUR PURSUIT OF SUCCESS.

Failure is the Sage of Greatness. If we allow our faults and failures to teach us, we have then at that moment begun to unleash greatness by learning from them. You cannot be great without your own list of personal and professional failures. I don't know what your failures are, but I have my own long list. What I do know is that many of you who are reading this have allowed your faults and failures to suppress your greatness. Some of you have allowed decades-old mistakes to hold you captive as you live in a world of regret.

If that is you, I want you to listen to the Sage of Greatness as it speaks to you. There is no positive purpose in continually beating yourself up and hitting yourself over the head with past mistakes, regardless of their magnitude. There is no benefit to living your life looking in the rearview mirror, myopically obsessed with your past. The past is the past, so leave the pain and shame of your mistakes in the rearview mirror while making the choice to learn the lessons they can teach you.

A few years ago I was reeling and dealing with my mid-life funk. For those of you who have journeyed through the mid-life weirdness or are going through it now, you understand the fog that I am talking about; it is thick, confusing, and absolutely maddening.

I tried navigating out of it myself, but after numerous unsuccessful attempts I knew I needed the help of a wise and seasoned sage, a person who had insight and understanding that I did not have myself, and one who could help me make sense of it all. I hired an executive coach who was twenty years older than me. He was well acquainted with the funk of midlife, and he knew how to help me get through it. I have given him the title of Saggio (the Latin form of Sage). He had answers for my questions, he had solutions for my problems, he had wisdom for my ignorance, and he had patience for my journey. I owe him more than I will ever be able to repay, for he truly changed my life. Saggio was my tutor, mentor, and wise counselor who guided me through the funk and fog of life.

There is another Sage that has been with me throughout my life and has been with you as well. It is the Sage of Greatness. The Sage of Greatness has been reaching out to you, speaking to you, calling you, and attempting to teach you. In every failure, every misstep, every blunder, and every fumbled attempt, the Sage of Greatness has been there for all of us.

The Sage of Greatness has a few things to teach us that can and will instantaneously change our lives if we will listen. Resoundingly and with the volume turned up, the Sage of Greatness teaches us to stop looking at life through the rearview mirror of regret and look with hope and expectancy through the front windshield of promise and opportunity. The Sage of Greatness speaks to help us navigate the devastation of personal failures and professional missteps. This Sage gently coaches us and tutors us along each step so that we can live our lives fully and unleash the greatness of our potential. The Sage of Greatness keeps nudging us to focus only on what is ahead and to let the past fade, not in regret but in gratitude. Every failure, every struggle, and every difficulty, are gifts given to us rather than unfortunate events that happened to us. The Sage of Greatness will show us how to be grateful and how to turn ashes into something truly magnificent.

For a short season, I had gone through a stretch of making one bad leadership decision after another. As we finally turned the corner from that embarrassing stint, I was left to deal with my own shame and blame. I kept my eyes locked on the rearview mirror of regret and self-loathing. It took me quite a while before I turned my eyes back to the front windshield of opportunity. It's easy to adjust our eyes to focus on what went wrong in the past and lose sight of the good that is coming right in front of us. The Sage of Greatness is doing everything it can to teach us not to focus on what's behind, but, instead, learn from it and readjust our vision forward so that we can fully unleash greatness on the world. The Sage of Greatness has wisdom to impart that will help us make those mistakes only once, gaining every ounce of insight that is possible for a better and brighter future.

GRATITUDE IS ESSENTIAL TO LEANING INTO GREATER SUCCESS AFTER DEALING WITH DISAPPOINTMENT AND FAILURE.

Here's the core message we must listen to and live by: Stop living in the past. Instead, learn from it, let it go, and move on. This is by far one of the biggest limitations that holds so many people prisoner. While there is often profound pain attached to our past, there is no value or benefit in reliving it and repeatedly reminding ourselves of what went wrong or who did what or what wasn't right. Those who choose to live in the past, reliving their failures or nursing injustices, have shackled themselves to something that can never be changed.

I recently spoke for an organization that had gone through some traumatic leadership challenges where there was abuse of power and mistreatment of people. There was obvious pain attached to their past and many were holding tightly to it. No one denies the poor leadership that caused the pain; it is what it is, it was what it was. But to continue living in that pain serves no positive purpose. There is no value in allowing what once happened to negatively affect our current well-being or our future success.

LET GO OF YOUR PAST PAIN SO THAT YOU CAN MOVE FORWARD TO A GREATER STORY.

The Sage of Greatness begs us to let go of our past pain so that we can move forward to a greater story and success. You may find yourself realizing that you have held tightly to past failure or injustice and now it's time to let it go.

There are things you cannot change. There are things that will never be made right. There are things that cannot be undone. Do yourself and everyone else a favor; let it go, and move on.

Your failure is not fatal, nor is it final. I know you may want to argue with me right now, and tell me that your failure was so epic that it caused you and others a lot of pain and embarrassment, and your unique failure is both fatal and final. I am not dismissing that there are varying degrees of failure, and that sometimes we blow it in epic ways, but, in reality, the only failures that are fatal or final are the ones we allow to have permanent power over us.

When we assign that level of power to our failures, we will forever live under the oppressive thumb of regret and shame. Regret and shame are destructive forces that, if left unresolved, will derail our present pursuit of success and more importantly will squeeze the life out of you.

The path to freeing yourself from this limitation is forgiveness. Forgiveness is an amazing gift to experience and to give. I have found that the hardest person to forgive is myself. I have had some people do me dirty through the years, but forgiving them was far easier than forgiving myself.

ONE OF THE GREATEST ACTS OF SELFLESSNESS IS SELF-FORGIVENESS.

You may be where I have been a time or two, giving yourself a beat down for what you did or didn't do; what you allowed or didn't allow; what you said or didn't say. Let me ask you this question: what good has come from the self-loathing and self-punishment you have engaged in for the mistakes of your past? How has that helped you or those around you?

LEAVE YOUR SHAME AND REGRET AND LIVE A NEW LIFE WITH DEEPER GRATITUDE AND GREATER WISDOM.

I am not suggesting that you gloss over your mistakes. The fact is that you absolutely need to own them and in the cases where you can make them right, you should. What I am saying is that if you are still breathing and on the top side of dirt, then your failures are not fatal nor final.

If your career or marriage ended, or people got hurt, or your dream crashed, you can recover; there is hope. It may not feel like it at the moment, but if you will receive and give forgiveness, to yourself and others, you can leave your shame and regret and live a new life with deeper gratitude and greater wisdom. The Sage of Greatness is committed to you; you must listen to its wisdom and lean into your greatness!

To fully process this chapter, I want you to intentionally think through these questions. Do yourself a favor and take the time to answer them so that you can leave the past behind and embrace the exciting present and future. There may be some pain associated with your answers, but on the other side of your pain is forgiveness and hope:

1. What failures have I allowed to define my life?

_____

_____

_____

2. What inglorious parts of my past do I let hold me prisoner in my present?

_____

_____

_____

3. What shame or regret do I need to release?

_____

_____

_____

4. What do I need to forgive myself or somebody else for?

_____

_____

_____

5. What can I learn from my failures?

_____

_____

_____

6. How am I going to specifically apply the wisdom of the Sage of Greatness to create a bigger and better future?

_____

_____

_____

THE ROAR

THERE WAS A LION who once roared. He was the king of the jungle, and he prowled and pounced with fierce strength. He ruled his kingdom with resolve. He was mighty and fearless, until one day when he was taken captive and caged. He fought to flex his muscles and demonstrate his strength, but the cage was unyielding. He roared with ferocious intensity, making threats with every grunt and growl.

Crowds came to see his power on display and stood in awe of his greatness, but time in captivity began to take its toll on him. The lion's roar began to wane until there was no more roar. He lost his heart, lost his confidence and along with those, he lost his roar. He was left to finish his days in a sad state of demoralized, powerless existence. He forgot what it meant to be a lion, and he forgot what it was like to roar.

Something happened to me the day I turned forty. It was the day I started living in fear. We had just finished a building project that propelled the organization we founded into a whole new sphere of impact and influence. We were growing in size and reach like never before.

FEAR IS CRUEL, MERCILESS, AND RUTHLESS.

From a professional perspective it was a dream come true. From a personal perspective it became a nightmare of fear that I would live with for years.

A friend of mine made a site visit to see the new facilities, and he, like most, was impressed with what we had built and the reach of our organization, and he celebrated our success.

I remember opening my heart to him as we walked and talked through the building. "I'm afraid we are going to lose it all. I don't know how to maintain our growth. I don't know how we sustain our success. I am afraid this is going to come to a screeching halt!"

He looked at me like I was an idiot, because that's what good friends do. He immediately responded, "You are not going to lose anything. You are not going backward. You are not going to fail." As much as I wanted to believe him, I instead listened to the voice of fear that controlled me.

For the next two years we grew exponentially. The impact of our organization was felt regionally and everything on the surface seemed strong. Internally, however, I was paralyzed and imprisoned by fears, and they became self-fulfilling prophecies. At the pinnacle of success and what should have been days filled with celebration and joy, I was consumed with doubts and fears. I leashed myself to fear, insecurity, and self-defeating thoughts.

Over the next few months and years we went from exponential growth, to marginal growth, to no growth, and then to decline—all due primarily to my personal fears of losing everything. My leadership during that period of time was not awesome. I had become indecisive, panicked, and "zombified"; I epitomized the walking dead. My fears overwhelmed every thought and move and everyone around me suffered for it. I had lost heart and consequently I had lost hope. I was enslaved to fear, and fear is a cruel slave master. Fear shows no mercy, no compassion, no understanding, no grace. Fear is cruel, shameless, and merciless; it held me captive for seven long years.

LEAVE YOUR FEARS AND FIND YOUR ROAR.

For a time, I was that caged lion who had lost its roar, but fortunately I found my heart and began to roar again. As I first began to recognize and then resist the grip that fear had on me, I found inner resolve and strength again. As I refused to listen to the voices of doubt and inadequacy, a bold confidence resurrected deep within me.

I was leaving my life of fear behind. I had been in an abusive relationship with fear for years, and I was done with getting the life kicked out of me by it. I was not going to be held captive anymore. I wanted my freedom to flex my muscles and roar again.

Since then my life has been renewed; I am a freed man. It's not that I don't have the influence of fear continually breathing down my neck; it's that I have chosen a new way to live. I've chosen to live courageously and from a place of inner strength. I've chosen to lead from a perspective of faith and belief in what could be and should be. Fear knocked the wind out of me for a few years, but that was then. This is who I am now; confident, courageous, bold, daring—a man on a mission to unleash greatness on the world.

LIVE COURAGEOUSLY AND FROM A PLACE OF INNER STRENGTH.

The pursuit of greatness should scare you a bit, but you cannot let fear stop you. I have sat with many people who shared their stories and who were unaware that their limiting factor was their fear. I have sat in the front row as executives allowed a low ceiling of performance and growth due to their hidden insecurities. For you to unleash greatness on the world, you must let go of what cannot be explained or reasoned or proven and take the leap. The life you are looking for, the leader you were meant to be, and the success you dream of is found in courage, bravery, and bold action.

Once you are able to identify and understand your fears, you can call them out and begin to face them. The only way to combat fear so that you move from disadvantage to advantage is head on. Believe that impossibilities can become possible, trust that good things are coming your way, and take courageous steps into uncertainty.

You may be where I was, caged and imprisoned by fear, doubts, and insecurities. If this is where you find yourself, it no longer has to be your story. Awaken fierce courage and get your roar back. I dare you to roar again. The world needs you to find the powerful qualities of your life and leadership and for you to be unleashed.

DON'T LET YOUR FEARS AND INSECURITIES KEEP YOU FROM THE LIFE YOU WANT.

There was a movie documentary released in the 70's called *On Any Sunday*. It showcased the world of motor bikes, dirt bikes, and pure and simple adrenaline-driven fun. That movie had an impact on me that has stuck with me all these years. It birthed in me a desire to experience the world of motorcycles for myself. It took me more than thirty years to finally purchase my own motorcycle, and it was everything I had dreamed it would be.

The dirt bike of choice for me after months of testing, searching, and selecting was the Honda CRF 450. The CRF 450 is a beast of a bike with muscle, power, agility, and speed. The bike was designed to be a full-throttle, high-performance machine that would take you virtually anywhere you have the brass to go. After purchasing my bike, I ran into an old acquaintance who rode as well. We started talking about the sport when he shared with me the most valuable insight to dirt-bike riding. He said, "This is not going to make sense now, but it will when you're out riding. The answer to almost everything in dirt-biking is throttle. If you get into trouble, hit the throttle. If your bike gets squirrelly in the sand, twist the grip and throttle up. Get comfortable throttling that engine; it will keep you safe and out of trouble."

I was an inexperienced rider at the time and my brain was telling me that his logic seemed exactly the opposite, illogical. When I got into trouble on the trails, the last thing I wanted to do was speed up. However, when I overrode my fear instincts, I realized he was right. Your best friend when you are riding is your ability to throttle that engine beyond your comfort zone; you've got to let that engine roar. Before long, I fell in love with the throttle. I loved the roar of the engine. I am an adrenaline junkie by nature and have experienced various forms of adrenaline inducers, but I have to say that hitting the throttle and letting the engine roar is beyond exhilarating. To state the obvious, the immediate result of hitting the throttle is rapid acceleration. The throttle gets your wheels turning and gets you moving. Dirt-bike riding taught me a few things about life and leadership but most importantly it taught me this: get comfortable with twisting the grip, letting it rip, and throttling up!

The reason you are reading this book, at least in part, is due to your desire to hit the throttle of your life and accelerate your opportunity and success. I can tell you that for me the thrill of personal and professional achievement far outweighs the adrenaline rush of any extreme sport. Though adrenaline created by death-defying activities is certainly a rush, nothing compares to taking your life to new places of personal growth and professional achievement. When I am accelerating my personal and professional opportunities, I feel fully alive. It's at those moments that I taste the purpose of my life; accelerating opportunity is a big part of unleashing greatness.

THE SUCCESS YOU WANT IS ON THE OTHER SIDE OF LETTING YOUR LEADERSHIP-ENGINE ROAR.

Think about your current story: how are you currently engaging the throttle? If you are keeping it tame and middle-of-the-road, then it is likely that it is comparable to the measure of success you are currently experiencing. If you want more success, more achievement, and more opportunity, then the only way to see those become reality is to overcome your fears by hitting the throttle, and hitting it hard.

I know your brain and probably some good-willed people are going to do everything they can to keep you at low rpm's and suggest that you play it safe, don't go overboard, avoid extremes, don't go too far. In large part those who try to influence you in that way are likely to be people who have not experienced significant levels of achievement, or what they have was given to them. If you are sitting back and waiting for opportunity to knock, you are going to get bored, and years of your life are going to pass by, leaving you to wonder what happened. Forget waiting; let's get busy and throttle up. Get your wheels spinning and see where you can go and what you can do. Being unleashed is about being intentional and sometimes even utilizing irrational acceleration that will most often scare you. It's about you deciding to get comfortable with what makes you uncomfortable. It's about you choosing to break the sound barrier and go faster than you've gone before.

In the introduction I highlighted two essential keys of success: commitment and intensity. Remember this, your commitment will determine your success. Your intensity will determine the speed of your success. The key insight that I want you to capture in this chapter is the strategic advantage of *intensity*. Intensity is about marshaling every ounce of your emotional, physical, and mental energy and laser-focusing it to dominate the invisible force field that is limiting your pursuit of success. What intensity also means is that you are totally dedicated and going all out, giving your very best to live and lead from advantage.

ARE YOU TOTALLY DEDICATED AND GOING ALL OUT, GIVING YOUR VERY BEST TO LIVE AN EXTRAORDINARY LIFE?

Take a minute to assess your intensity. On a scale from 1 to 10, 1 meaning the engine is on but only at an idle and 10 meaning a full-throttle maximized effort, what's your current level of intensity? Use the scale below to mark where you believe you are right now. For this to have any value for you, it's important to be honest with yourself and place the mark where your intensity is actually operating and not where you want it to be or know it needs to be.

0 1 2 3 4 5 6 7 8 9 10

As I write this book, my son is in the midst of launching a new business. I recently sat with him to talk through some strategies that will help him set up his new venture for success. I asked him two primary questions: How committed to this are you? And what level of intensity are you going to put forth to drive this to succeed? His immediate response was a level-9 intensity. I asked him why his 9 wasn't a 10, and he gave a reasonable answer; however, I wanted to know why he wasn't going all out with intensity. I have launched four organizations over the past twenty-plus years and I know the intensity that is required to be successful. The only number that gets the kind of results I was looking for was a level-10 maximized effort. As I challenged him to move his intensity from a 9 to a 10, he asked me to help him understand the difference.

Just a couple of years ago my son competed in a few desert races on his dirt bike. Even though he lacked the experience of most of the other competitors, he advanced quickly in the competitions and won several races. His last race was a seventy-five-mile circuit race, and Austin killed it. From the start of the race through each lap and across the finish line, Austin shredded the course and dominated the other riders in his bracket. To help him understand the difference between a level-9 intensity and level-10, I asked him a simple question: "Son, when you were racing, did you hit the throttle with level-9 intensity or level-10? Did you win races because you were a level-9 intensity or level-10?"

His immediate response was, "I was a level-10 intensity, full throttle the entire race."

And I responded, "That's exactly what it takes to win in life and business—all-in, all-out intensity!"

Level-10 intensity is about fully directing your physical, emotional, and mental energy toward the direction of your dreams. It is to give your very best effort and full attention to your pursuits and endeavors. Level-10 is your personal equivalent of leading and executing with full-throttle determination. Level-10 is the laser focus you bring to winning.

WHEN YOU FULLY ENGAGE YOUR MENTAL, PHYSICAL, AND EMOTIONAL ENERGY, YOU CREATE GAME-CHANGING MOMENTUM.

I have observed numerous people in their frustration questioning why things were not developing as quickly as they wanted or why it seemed like they were at a standstill. In most cases, the problem and solution were issues of intensity. They wanted epic success but without the epic effort that is required. Level-10 intensity is about investing all-out effort and maximum energy into your pursuits and endeavors in order to accelerate your success trajectory.

You may find yourself stuck and frustrated right now and looking for the answer to propel your life and leadership forward. Your answer may very well be found by increasing your intensity, letting your engine roar, and hitting the throttle. Taking it easy and idling your engine will get you limited results, and definitely not epic results. It's time for you to do what may be uncomfortable—to rev up your engine and hit the throttle of intensity. When you increase your intensity you will begin to see your story change from disadvantage and struggle to energized and activated greatness where you break through your barriers and limitations and achieve your dreams.

I want you to think through your story and take a personal inventory of what fears, doubts, inadequacies and insecurities may be holding you in their grip. Don't be afraid to answer these questions honestly:

1. What do you fear the most and how is it keeping you from an extraordinary life?

_____

_____

_____

2. What creates anxiety for you?

_____

_____

_____

_____

3. What is it that paralyzes you with uncertainty?

_____

_____

_____

_____

4. What is your worst nightmare come true?

_____

_____

_____

_____

5. What is keeping you from taking bold action?

_____

_____

_____

_____

_____

6. Who or what is keeping you from full-throttle living?

_____

_____

_____

_____

_____

THE VOICES

I WAS SITTING IN A leadership meeting a couple of years ago and was sharing a few stories from my experiences when one of the gang chimed in, "Jerome, you have lived a thousand lives." I had never thought of it in those terms, but he framed an underlying driver that has been deep below the surface of my life for as long as I can remember. I have always been inclined to adventure, entrepreneurship, travel, risky endeavors, and things that scare the stuffing out of you. Somewhere along the way, I picked up a profound and unquenchable curiosity.

I want to see how things work, experience cultures that are far removed from my own, and attempt things I have never tried. In simple form, I want to live my life to its fullest. I hope you have a similar curiosity.

KNOWING WHICH VOICES TO LISTEN TO IS AN ESSENTIAL PRACTICE THAT WILL ACCELERATE YOUR LIFE, LEADERSHIP AND PURSUITS.

It never ceases to amaze me how people try to discourage people like us and influence us to pursue lesser dreams, smaller goals, and diminished pursuits. It's as if they believe their idea of a safe, risk-free life is the way everyone should live, and so they determine to influence us to lose altitude and live for very safe dreams and ambitions.

If they want to live that way, that's their business; my life cannot be reduced to someone else's expectations or preferences. I cannot live someone else's life or conform to the image they believe I should. It's baffling to watch the attempts of some to do everything they can to minimize the dreams, hopes, and desires of others. I have found myself held prisoner by other people's voices of approval or opinion. This is where many people shrink and fall back; they listen to the wrong voices.

We are bombarded with a variety of discouraging voices every day: voices of shame, blame, regret, judgment, doubt, and criticism to name a few. It took me more years than I want to admit to realize I had allowed the wrong voices to take deep root in my brain and soul. I listened to the wrong people and consequently their voices overwhelmed the voices that really mattered, and I suffered for it.

You never know the real motive behind some of your critics. Is it jealousy, or fear, or competition? Some of them don't even know how toxic their comments are. Many mean well, but they still cause harm. Knowing which voices to listen to is an essential practice that will accelerate your life, leadership and pursuits. Listening to the right voices will fuel your success, empower your boldness, and enlarge your expectations of what is yet to come.

The question you must consider is this: Are you listening to the right voices? Do you have the right people speaking into your life right now? Which voices do you need to eliminate immediately? Which voices do you need to bring into your life to help you accelerate into the life you were meant for?

I need to tell you about a friend of mine, Jeff McManus. Jeff and I became friends at a speakers' event in Atlanta just a couple of years ago. There was an immediate, unexpected friendship that developed and has become a high-value relationship for me. Jeff is one of the most encouraging and optimistic people I know. Every time we have a conversation he says the right thing at the right time, EVERY TIME!

Jeff has become a voice that I value and trust. I seek his counsel and insight, and he provides the added benefit of the encouraging words I need to help me overcome the insecurities and defeating thoughts that I sometimes let get the best of me.

The pursuit of greatness and success is not a road for the weak; it's a journey that requires you to find a few people who will be the right voices to help you stay the course and prevail. One of the most strategic steps to take in the pursuit of greatness is to wisely select your traveling companions. Your traveling companions are people who more than anything become a centering voice that propel you to greater success and more frequent victories like Jeff has been for me.

ARE YOU LISTENING TO THE RIGHT VOICES?

I want to give you a filtering process to help identify the right people you should allow to speak into your life and leadership greatness. These have all come through my experiences of making both the right and wrong choices regarding the people I have listened to through the years. This is a practical and common sense approach, but it is often ignored and dismissed. Follow this process and you will find the right voices who will help propel you to new heights of achievement and success.

1. Listen to people who see your potential and are not jealous of your success.

It should go without saying, but the words of jealous people are destructive and often subversive. It can take some time to discern their ultimate motive, but even though they give you positive affirmations, their heart envies and despises your growth, development, and achievements.

Over the course of time they will sit like a viper waiting to bite you and inject their jealous venom into your bloodstream. A key practice in selecting the right people is to listen to more than their words; listen to their heart. Words can often deceive, but the heart is difficult to hide.

2. Listen to people who want you to succeed and who celebrate your rise to the top.

I know I have found a candidate who I can trust to speak into my life by whether or not they sincerely celebrate my successes. It is a refreshing voice that not only celebrates each step forward but also champions my success journey. Your journey forward and onward will require the fuel of people who celebrate your growth, development, and achievements. People who truly champion you will be vital links to your ability to lean into greatness.

3. Listen to people who speak encouraging words that breathe life into you and your dreams.

I love having conversations with dreamers. Their dreams seem to give life to my dreams. Their positive conversation gives hope to my aspirations. Dreamers bring optimism to challenges and bring inspiration to the demands and dilemmas of life. In its purest definition, encouragement means to give courage. This is a cherished gift to receive from the right voices as the journey of greatness is a demanding one and can discourage us along the way. To have someone "giving us courage" is a priceless treasure that is essential to achieving an extraordinary life.

4. Listen to people who are pursuing success themselves.

When I interact with someone who is pursuing success they have my full attention. I want to learn what they know. I want to listen intently to what I can garner from their experience. I want to identify solutions they are discovering in their struggle toward success. The vital point here is that they are in the game for themselves and not armchair quarterbacking someone else's game.

They have blood, sweat, mud, and tears just like I do, and I respect their input.

5. Listen to people who are positive, upbeat, and who have a greatness mindset.

Words have a very close relationship with the Law of Attraction. What you say, you attract. The words you speak have a way of creating the very truth you are speaking to or from. Words are powerful! You can quickly discern a person's perspective simply by listening to them for a few minutes. Their words will quickly reveal their perspective. Often times it's not just the words but the energy behind their words. Negativity is destructive. Small thinking is destructive. Find people who think big and speak positively and optimistically.

6. Listen to people who speak the truth in love and who have no agenda except to help you win.

A key voice that is essential to your success is to have someone or, even better, several people who can tell you the truth you need to hear but who say it in such a way that you do not question their motives. Everyone needs truth tellers in their life, but we do not need to hear everyone's truth about us. We each have blind spots that go undetected in our lives. This is where the right people who have the right voice are so important. They can lovingly, but directly reveal the truth that we need to hear and can deliver it in a way that we can receive it.

When you have someone who is helping you see things you have been blind to and you know their agenda is to help, you have found a trusted voice, so listen to them! Ask them probing questions that will help you drill deep into what you do not understand and cannot see for yourself.

7. Listen to people who have experienced the kind of success you hope to achieve.

I have become a raving fan of Verne Harnish, CEO of Gazelles, a global, business-growth company that is focused on helping professionals scale their business for success. I was first introduced to Verne at the National Speakers Association Influence Conference in 2015 where he was one of the keynote presenters. I put Verne's presentation in the top five best business speeches I have ever experienced.

Everything about Verne is appealing to me. He is an exceptional speaker who delivers practical yet profound content that I can relate to and implement. He is leading a very successful global company and I aspire to do the same. He is continually growing and developing and looking for new solutions to help him lead his enterprises to new levels of success; he has fresh insights that I can learn from. He is living internationally (in Barcelona, Spain) and enjoying the life he is creating for himself and his family, and that's what I want as well. Because his success relates directly to what I am endeavoring to create, he has a voice in my pursuits. Even though I don't have a direct line to Verne, I can read his books, listen to him speak, follow his social media, and continually receive strategic investments that are changing the game for me. Who is this voice for you?

8. Listen to people who have failed and who have picked themselves up and kept going.

Nothing speaks louder than someone who has tried, failed, and then kept trying until they succeed. I have a total respect for people who openly talk about their mistakes and who have proven they were students of their failures rather than prisoners. If I have learned anything about success, it almost always takes several failed attempts to get it right.

Leaders who walk with a limp because they lost a battle or two are leaders who can be trusted. The reality is that someone else's failure can help me not only overcome my own failures, but can help me avoid many other failures.

I don't sit in judgment of people who have failed, for I have a long list myself. I respect them for trying and learning everything they can from their painful experience.

Failure is one of the greatest mentors in a leader's life, so welcome it and learn everything you can from those who have failed in their journey as well. The simple fact is that there is far more to learn in failure than outright success. Failure is a clear stepping stone on the path and process to greatness.

9. Listen to people whose hearts and motives are pure.

There is really nothing I value more than someone whose heart is pure, free of deceit and malice, and one that is not jaded by the injustices of life. I have already mentioned that the heart reveals itself quickly. You can tell the condition of someone's heart by simply listening to the words they speak. When someone's heart and motives are pure you can trust the insight and wisdom they share and can rest assured they want the best for you.

10. Listen to people who energize you and lift you to new heights.

I am writing this on a flight from Ixtapa Zihuantanejo, Mexico where I spoke at the North American Congress on Tourism. Following my presentation, one of the attendees approached me to thank me for the investment I made in her life and leadership.

Her name is Araceli Ramos Rosaldo, the Director of Public Promotions and Relations for Jose Cuervo Tequila. She is an engaging and energized individual. When she speaks you can't help but feel her passion, zest for life, and focused energy as they transfer to you. There's a reason she is the spokesperson for Jose Cuervo, and it is that she energizes people!

In our post-conference dialogue, her energy and enthusiasm fueled my dreams and vision of what could and should be. She is exactly the kind of person you want to have speak into your life—the kind of person who brings energy, encouragement, and enthusiasm. This is important to your success because you will deal with plenty of people who will de-energize and demotivate you. The right people saying the right things will change the game for you.

THERE IS POWER BEHIND THE WORDS OF OTHERS THAT CAN CATAPULT SOMEONE'S LIFE TO NEW DIMENSIONS OF SUCCESS OR LEAD THEM TO FRUSTRATION AND FAILURE.

The voices we listen to cannot be underestimated. There is power behind the words of others that can catapult someone's life to new dimensions of success or lead them to frustration and failure. A key discipline is to make yourself keenly aware of the voices that are influencing you.

Through many heartaches, I have learned some valuable lessons as to the people I allow to speak into my life. While I can learn from my worst enemy, I will NEVER again let the voice of those who are against me influence the trajectory of my life. I am teachable, but I get to choose who I will be taught by.

I passed through the neighborhood that I grew up in the other day and slowly drove past my childhood home. Not a whole lot has changed over forty years; however, going back in time was surreal. We lived on a corner with two sides of our house exposed to the street. I first drove past the front of the house, and memories began to flood my thoughts. I remembered days of slip-and-slides, green machine races, mulberry and cottonwood tree climbing, skateboard crashes, lemonade stands, and the normal neighborhood mischief. As I turned the corner and rounded the side of the house, my fondest childhood memories gripped me, so much so that I slowed the car to a stop.

Flashbacks of conversations with my dad were as real as if time had stood still. I cherish those late evening chats I had with my dad as we sat stargazing under the cottonwood tree in our backyard. The New Mexico skies in the 70's were like a private planetarium with the most amazing views of satellites, stars, galaxies, constellations and other heavenly sites. There were many nights in the summer when my dad and I would talk about life; we would dream great dreams, we would tell epic stories while counting the crossing satellites.

What I could not have understood back then was what was taking place in me. I am not sure my dad even knew what he was doing, but he was giving me a gift. He gave me the gift of dreaming—the gift of what could be and should be. He gave me the gift of seeing into a preferred future of the life that I could create and who and what I could become. There's no question in my mind that those formative years in my life birthed greatness in me. He gave me an amazing gift, the gift of believing in the potential of my life. He gave me the dream to live an epic story.

GREATNESS IS BIRTHED IN THOUGHTS AND IMAGINATIONS THAT CREATE DESIRE AND THEN ACTION.

Twenty years ago I lost my father to leukemia. I would give anything for only one more night in that swing in our backyard. I would tell him in detail the story of my life, and then I would thank him for helping me see that greatness was waiting to be unleashed on the world through me. He gave me a profound gift, the ability to believe in what could be. I was given permission to dream of a better way and a better life. My thoughts were not constrained to the confines of reality or resources or anything for that matter. He taught me to believe, and I still do, that greatness is one fulfilled dream away, but that of course must start with a dream.

Greatness is birthed in thoughts and imaginations that create desire and then action.

I want to give you the very gift my father gave me—the gift to dream. Some of you reading this right now did not have someone like my father who fueled your dreams from an early age. In fact, I suspect that many of you have had quite the opposite experience. You very likely had, and maybe still do, someone who perpetually poured water on the flames of your dreams. They are the ones I call the "Dousers." I am certain you recognize Mr. and Mrs. Douser, they are everywhere and in abundance.

DON'T LET THOSE WHO DOUSE DREAMS EXTINGUISH THE FIRE OF YOUR DREAMS AND DESIRES.

Mr. and Mrs. Douser are sometimes good people intending good, but causing harm. They can also be very bad people who are being destructive intentionally. The "Trying to Protect You Dousers" are most often controlled by their own fears; they are scared to death that if you attempt to achieve greatness you might fall short or fail. They believe that the risk far outweighs the reward, and they seek to keep you safe from harm and free from pain. They are typically good people, meaning good, but nonetheless dousing your dreams.

Then there are the Sinister and Selfish Dousers who most often are driven by envy and jealousy. They will do anything and everything at their disposal to dissuade and discourage you and, if possible, extinguish your flame.

I have had my fair share of interactions with these types of Dousers. Some are blatant and brutal; they have no regard for decency, honor, and respect. They are so filled with envy and jealousy that they will lie, cheat and steal to derail your pursuit of greatness.

There are really only two things I have to say about this type of Douser: First, don't listen to them nor let them cause you to dumb your greatness down—not for a second! They are not worth your time, so do not give them any space in your brain. Secondly, you have a middle finger for a reason, and these Dousers are the perfect people to use it on. The sooner you tell the Evil Dousers to take a flying leap off a very tall cliff, the sooner you will be able to get on with your pursuit of greatness. You don't need their approval or permission; just leave them in your dust.

When you open your thoughts and imagination to the possibilities of greatness, this is the very moment you will begin to unleash your greatness on the world. Do yourself a favor, and take a few minutes to think through how you might be allowing the Doubting or Devilish Dousers to keep you tethered to a lame and tame life. It's time to call them out, shut them down, and get on with the life you were meant to live—a life of unleashed greatness.

I shared the story of the Dousers with a friend of mine at the cigar shop a couple of days ago. He immediately asked me if I had had anyone like that in my life. The quick and easy answer is: "Of course!"

The long, painful answer is that I have more than a few of them, and I have unfortunately allowed some of them to distract me from my pursuits. If you are attempting to do anything of any magnitude, you will have Dousers doing whatever they can to knock you off course.

WHEN YOU OPEN YOUR THOUGHTS AND IMAGINATION TO THE POSSIBILITIES OF GREATNESS THIS IS THE VERY MOMENT YOU WILL BEGIN TO UNLEASH YOUR GREATNESS ON THE WORLD.

I want you to think through the positive and negative voices you have had in your life. As you reflect, begin to identify the tactics of those who were set to douse your dreams and your drive:

1. What is the common tactic used to distract or derail you?

_____

_____

_____

_____

2. What is the consistent thread of behavior that those who may intend good, but are actually causing harm, exhibit?

_____

_____

_____

_____

3. Why do you think you are giving the dousers permission to negatively influence you?

_____

_____

_____

_____

The world is filled with both doubting and devilish dousers. They are everywhere and are not going away. The point I am making is not necessarily to get you to eliminate them from your life, but for you to identify how they are affecting you, and then to encourage you to stay your course and keep your determined resolve. On the other hand, you may have one or more devilish dousers in your life that you will need to distance yourself from in order to achieve your dreams. Take the time to weigh their impact on you and, if necessary, to get them out of your life immediately.

DREAM EPIC DREAMS AND THEN DO EVERYTHING YOU CAN TO MAKE THEM COME TRUE.

A key strategy that I have embraced to help me see greater possibilities and to help me stay focused on pursuing an epic life has been to surround myself with "the right people." The right people are people like my father who spoke into my life and encouraged me to dream and to dream big. The right people are those who encourage you and who want you to succeed as much or more than you want you to succeed.

The right people not only fuel your dreams, they also bring wise counsel and advice as you lean into greatness.

They only want you to live your life to its fullest, and they celebrate you.

When you have the right people speaking into your story, you write a greater story for your life. The right people also know how to help you reject the voice and opinion of Mr. and Mrs. Douser so that you keep your course and stand tall.

DON'T UNDERESTIMATE THE POWER OF SELF-TALK.

I want for you more than anything to find in this book the voice of encouragement and the tools needed for you to create the life you want and for you to allow your deepest dreams to consume you, so much so that you pursue them with all that you've got. I long to see you break free from the opinions and constraints of the wrong people so that you can be encouraged and inspired by the right people. I want to be that gift to you that my father was to me. I want you to dream epic dreams and then do everything you can to make them come true.

There is one more voice that I want to bring into the spotlight, and that is your own voice. If we could only record and then play back the myriad of things we say to ourselves. Often the worst and most damaging critics are not the voices or opinions of others, but our own voices with our own words that we speak over our own lives. This voice carries more weight than any other.

As I was making every effort to navigate through a difficult season in my life, I read a book that taught me how to talk to myself. I know this may sound strange, but you need to know what to say to yourself.

My self-talk had been toxic; I spoke destructive, defeating, demeaning, and degrading things over my own life. My voice was so loud and so convincing that I couldn't hear what others were saying. Once I recognized the unhealthy practice that I had been involved in, I began to make changes and the results were immediate.

WHEN YOU LISTEN TO THE RIGHT VOICES, YOUR LIFE AND LEADERSHIP EXPONENTIALLY ACCELERATE.

I began to exchange the negative and destructive self-talk with words of life and positive affirmation. I began to trade words of shame and condemnation for words of grace and forgiveness. I began to eliminate self-defeating words for words that gave me hope, expectancy, and life. I became intentionally aware of every word that I allowed my heart to whisper, and it changed everything. Don't underestimate the power of self-talk.

I still face occasional words that surface both internally and externally that try to subvert my efforts and pursuit of success, but as soon as I identify them, I change them and it changes me. When I am listening to the right voices, my life and leadership exponentially accelerate. When I have the right voices encouraging me, guiding me, and instructing me I am unstoppable. This is an area of a leader's life that must be regularly evaluated.

What you say to yourself is essential to achieving your dreams and unleashing your greatness. I am not talking about inflated statements that are egocentric, but strategic investments that strengthen and center us at the core of our being.

Your own self-talk may be the single greatest advantage to give yourself in your pursuit of success. It's one thing to listen to what others say, it's an entirely different issue of greater magnitude to speak the right words over your own life. You can change your life in an instant by applying the insights of this chapter. Think carefully through the following questions.

1. What specific things do you say to yourself that are positive and helpful?

_____

_____

_____

2. What specific things do you say to yourself that are negative and destructive?

_____

_____

_____

_____

3. What must change immediately about your self-talk?

_____

_____

_____

_____

4. Who are the people in your life that lift and build you up?

_____

_____

_____

_____

5. Who are the "Dousers" in your life that are speaking words of death, defeat, and discouragement?

_____

_____

_____

_____

6. What are the specific words you need to speak to yourself every day to fuel your success and pursuit of an extraordinary life?

_____

_____

_____

_____

THE QUESTION

WHEN YOU BREAK THE pursuit of success down, you will circle back to one of the most profound questions of life. It's a simple and yet complicated question that must be answered. Those who refuse to take the time to answer it are those who have chosen to live their lives far below their potential, leaving so much of what could be unrealized. The question goes far beyond hopes, dreams, and desires. It goes well below the surface of aspirations to a place that lies at the core of our being. It is the essential questions of true success and significance.

Let me ask the question directly: "What do you want?" This question is not as easy to answer as it seems on the surface. In reality, it takes time to process in order to do it justice. Part of the difficulty in answering this question is that we want a lot of things. We want to live in a certain kind of home, drive certain types of cars, eat certain types of food, enjoy certain types of vacations and experiences, and this is just the beginning of the list. To answer this question, I want you to go well below the surface of things and experiences to the more important dimension of quality of life.

WHAT PRECISELY DO YOU WANT?

If we keep our answers just to the tangible, material desires we will be in a perpetually never-ending pursuit. I have spent a good deal of time trying to answer this question by "medicating" myself with things that cannot satisfy. If you haven't discovered this for yourself yet, the desire for possessions is insatiable. You will always be hungry for more and left wanting if you merely attempt to answer this question with superficial stuff.

This question speaks to the truest desires of the heart and is attached to the very purpose of your life. Getting to the heart of what you really want will help you laser-lock your pursuits on those things that fuel your success. When you are able to answer this question with clarity and conviction, you will find the drivers, motivators, and accelerators that will jettison your life and leadership to new levels of achievement.

If you don't have a clear understanding of what you want, it is going to take you a long time, if ever, to arrive at the place that is deeply satisfying and meaningful. How you answer the question will determine whether you get to the place you truly want to be, filled with passion and purpose.

When I finally sat down and answered this question and took the time to weigh my answers with my truest desires, it led me to make a decision to transition my career. I was fueled with a clarity and confidence that empowered me to take a bold step and make a radical career change. I finally left the organization that I founded and led for fifteen years to pursue what is the truest desire of my heart. I am more alive now than I have ever been. I have greater joy and true contentment than I have ever known, and the impact of my life is expanding globally in profound ways.

KNOWING WHAT YOU WANT WITH CLARITY AND RESOLVE WILL FUEL COURAGEOUS ACTION IN THE DIRECTION OF AN EXTRAORDINARY LIFE.

To help you identify what it is that you really want, imagine that you are standing next to two trees. One tree has ripe, ready-for-picking fruit that is waiting for you to eat. The other has spoiled, rotten fruit that doesn't look desirable and consequently tastes just like it looks. The question has to be asked regarding how these two trees produce such vastly different fruit. On the surface there is no explanation. Everything above the surface looks the same; it's when you take a look below the surface that you see that the fruit of the tree is determined by the root system of the tree. To produce good fruit, you must cultivate good roots.

That's where the question we are drilling down on makes all the difference. What we want is answered first by the fruit we want to enjoy. Remember, don't think "stuff"; instead, think quality of life and purpose. When you are able to clearly know what you want, you then begin to do the root work that is critical to the fruit you desire. Getting to what you want, the fruit, reveals the root work.

In answering the primary question of what you want it's important to give yourself permission to dream the craziest, most outrageous dream that has no boundaries or limitations. You may want to think through your answer as a lifestyle architect or designer. When I first began to answer this question, it took me the better part of three to four months to distill it in such a way that it provided clarity and went beyond stuff and experiences. I have been in life and leadership development for twenty-five years, so I had a head start in the process, but what was different for me was that I was at an inflection point of life, redesigning a different future. In the first twenty-five years of my adult life, I was able to clearly understand what I loved to do and, to a degree, how I wanted to live. I was also very aware of what I didn't want to do and I made sure that what I didn't want and didn't enjoy were strategically removed from my future.

GIVE YOURSELF PERMISSION TO DREAM THE CRAZIEST, MOST OUTRAGEOUS DREAM THAT HAS NO BOUNDARIES OR LIMITATIONS.

As you drill down on this question, allow yourself to truly discover the deep desires and dreams of your heart. Once you mine those out and understand what they are, you can then design and create the future that belongs to you. Without this kind of clarity, you will find yourself aimlessly living your life and unquestionably frustrated by the self-imposed limitation of having no clear goal. Answering this question is an accelerator; it focuses your life and pursuits on what matters most.

Take some time to think through the following questions:

1. What specifically do you want? General answers to this question will only get you marginal results. It is vitally important to be precisely clear and specific.

_____

_____

_____

_____

_____

_____

2. How do you specifically define an extraordinarily great life?

_____

_____

_____

_____

_____

3. What specifically does your dream life look like, feel like, and taste like?

_____

_____

_____

_____

_____

4. What specifically is it going to be like when you achieve the life of your dreams?

_____

_____

_____

_____

5. What fruit do you want your life to produce?

_____

_____

_____

_____

When you have clarity, you can leap forward at warp speeds. When you know what you specifically and precisely want, you discover a hidden strength to stay your course and see your dreams come true, regardless of how steep the climb is.

I stopped in my tracks in awe as my daughter Lauren and I turned the corner on the path leading to the historic gateway of Machu Picchu village in Peru. I was captured in the moment by not only a bucket-list dream come true, but also by the sheer greatness of the endeavors of the Incas.

The Inca construction of Machu Picchu is beyond mind blowing. Machu Picchu is elevated 1000 ft. above the Urubamba River in a remote location in the Andes Mountains that would, by any human standards, seem impossible to forge anything from, especially an entire city. The overriding thought that immediately came to mind when seeing this city was, "How in the heck did they do this?" How did they build this fortified city atop an impossible rise in the subtropical region of the Andes? Let's go ahead and eliminate the possibility of alien assistance, as some have theorized, and take a look at reality.

The Incas were an impressive group of people who exhibited the qualities of greatness. They were disciplined and committed. This construction took time and a lot of it, but they stayed their course until it was completed. They had an amazing ability to carry the heavy weight of greatness. They built an empire the remains of which still exist today throughout South America. They demonstrated a resiliency that rivals any of the great civilizations of history. They lived from a place of dreams, hopes and aspirations. As my daughter and I walked a portion of the Inca Trail and meandered through the corridors and pathways of Machu Picchu, I saw evidence of a people that achieved greatness because of their ability to persevere and endure the demands of their pursuits.

WHEN YOU KNOW WHAT YOU WANT YOU CAN OVERCOME INSURMOUNTABLE BARRIERS.

The big question of Machu Picchu and other Inca developments is simply how? They did not have modern-day technology; they had no GPS, computer-assisted engineering, historical data or any of our modern equipment. What they set out to create is simply a fascinating and impressive feat that highlights human potential. As you walk through the corridors of this ancient city and touch the rocks that they laid by hand, you marvel at the perfected masonry and engineering genius they employed. They quarried all of the stones to build the city from massive natural stones, some bigger than houses. Our tour guide showed us how modern archaeologists believe the process of making the stones was accomplished. He explained that millions of stones were hewn by hand using only simple tools like magnetite, stone hammers, water and wooden sticks. Obviously they did not have explosives, jackhammers, drills, hydro-pressurized saws, diamond blades or the like. All they had was an uncanny ability and desire to carve this city from enormous white granite boulders into individual stones which have stood the test of time for 1500 years. What they really had was sheer determination and a ferocious tenacity to do what the vision demanded.

After we explored the city of Machu Picchu, our next jaunt would take us up to the actual peak of Machu Picchu Mountain at an elevation of 10,000 feet. It's hard to describe what we were looking at, but imagine a staircase going several thousand feet to the peak. It wasn't that clean and clear, but to get to the top one must scale 1726 steps of varying heights before reaching the summit. To say that it was steep does not do it justice. This was not a casual hike but rather a rigorous and steep ascent to the top. From where we were in the old city of Machu Picchu, we could see the tiny forms of those that made the trek before us in the distance. We were inspired to meet them at the top. Although inspired and optimistic, we were definitely not prepared for the climb. In fact, we didn't even know if our tickets permitted us to do so. We were not properly hydrated, nor did we have ample water to sustain us on the strenuous climb. In spite of what we didn't have, we chose to journey upward.

YOUR CLIMB TO A LIFE OF SIGNIFICANCE WILL REQUIRE DETERMINATION AND FEROCIOUS TENACITY TO ENDURE THE DEMANDS.

The climb was so arduous that we were very quickly questioning our decision to ascend to the peak. Lauren and I would go back and forth in our banter as to when we should turn around. Should we go to the top? Is it worth it? Haven't we seen enough? The redeeming part of the trek is that you stay in clear view of the peak virtually at all times. That helps and it hurts. There were times when the peak seemed further away, but then we would turn a corner and it seemed right on top of us. At best guess, we were about half way when we realized that one bottle of water was laughable, but there are no handy vendors on the side of this steep mountain waiting for us to drop in for a drink. We were both feeling the effects of the demanding climb and were seriously considering turning around.

There has always been a stubborn quality in me, whether for good or bad, that makes it very difficult for me to quit anything or to give up. Since we had made it at least half way, I just couldn't fathom turning around, so we journeyed on. Three quarters of the way up we were seriously hurting. We had rationed our water supply to a couple drops at a time to conserve what we could. We kept hoping the severe pitch of the trek would level out, but it never did. We wanted to give up countless times and many others on the journey did, but we didn't. We stayed the course and prevailed.

I clearly remember the final approach to the peak as the vistas of 15,000-foot peaks surrounded us. It was EPIC! The majesty of the moment and the grandeur of the Andes Mountains were worth every moment of strain and struggle. We stayed there for a bit just reveling not only in our accomplishment of the climb but also in the reward that the climb gave us.

From our perch atop of Machu Picchu Mountain, we could see for hundreds of miles. We saw seemingly endless views of snow-capped mountain peaks as well as the tropical Amazon basin below us where the fertile green vegetation covered steep, sloping foothills with big rivers. It was a moment well worth the price of admission.

If we had given up on the ascent, we would have missed the beauty of the mountaintop. There is a truism of life in this experience that I hope stays with me forever. The climb is worth it. The price of admission, although steep, pardon the pun, is worth it.

THE PRIZE IS AT THE TOP OF THE MOUNTAIN, AND IT AWAITS YOU WITH EXPECTANCY, ASKING YOU TO ACCEPT ITS INVITATION AND PAY ITS PRICE.

To maximize your performance and achieve what you dream of, you will be faced with the temptation of cutting your journey short and turning around midway. Before you make that decision, make sure you weigh the consequences. The prize is at the top of the mountain, and it awaits you with expectancy, asking you to accept its invitation and pay its price.

Take a minute to think through your journey and try to identify moments where you stepped back or maybe even walked away because of the pain you faced or the struggle of success. Try to be as specific as possible:

1. How are you trying to avoid the pain of your journey to success?

_____

_____

_____

2. When did you slow down or decide to take an easier path that delayed your success?

_____

_____

_____

_____

3. What success have you walked away from before it was fully realized because the price was too high?

_____

_____

_____

_____

4. What dreams do you need to revisit or reengage because you abandoned them due to the struggle?

_____

_____

_____

_____

5. What work do you need to get busy doing?

_____

_____

_____

_____

6. What mountains do you need to start climbing to create your success?

_____

_____

_____

_____

If you want to see your dreams come true, it's time to start climbing.

THE DRAFT

I HAVE VIVID MEMORIES OF fifth grade at Hawthorne Elementary School. Not only was I an "upper classman," I was about to graduate to mid-high school. Now I realize that graduating from fifth grade is not that big of a deal, but it sure felt like it then.

The highlight of every school year was in May when the physical education department put on the End of Year Olympics, and like the real Olympics, there was a wide variety of events to participate in. I didn't consider myself much of an athlete, but I wasn't afraid to put myself out there.

I remember participating in the long jump. I put my whole self into the competition and jumped as far as I could. I also participated in the hurdles, hundred-yard dash, and several other events. I dreamed of being the gold medalist. I had watched the real-deal Olympics when I was growing up, and I wanted to be a champion myself. I wish my grade school story was filled with memories of the glory of standing on the medalist podium, but that was not the case. I didn't win any medals, at least none that I can remember. I was all heart but not a lot of track-and-field talent.

What I remember most from the End of Year Olympic Games was one of the most amazing experiences that has remained vivid in my memory throughout the years. The event was the boys' four-hundred, one lap around the track. I wasn't the slowest kid in the class, nor was I the fastest, but I wanted to see what I could do. There were a dozen of us lined up for the race, and like thoroughbred race horses being held in the gate, we were ready to run and waiting for the coach to blow his whistle. Our coach finally gave the command, "Runners on your mark. Ready. Set." He blew the whistle and we were off, each of us running at full speed.

We made the first turn and I stayed with the lead group of runners. I was grinning from ear to ear. Something inside of me found incredible delight in this foot race.

The pack began to separate as we headed toward the second and final turn. Somehow, I held my pace and stayed with the guys up front. As we engaged the final turn, I had a sensation of being lifted; I literally felt light on my feet as we began to hit a speed that I could not explain. Mind you, we were boys running with hearts of Olympic champions. In our own minds we were among the greats running the grass fields at Hawthorne Elementary. As we approached the finish line, my body began to move faster than my feet knew how to maintain, so much so that I nearly lost my footing, but I somehow managed to stay upright. I was caught in the draft of the pack and their momentum and speed carried me.

THE PEOPLE YOU RUN WITH WILL DETERMINE THE RESULTS OF THE RACE.

I didn't win the race nor did I stand on the medalist podium, but what I experienced taught me something that I would later understand about life and leadership. There may be no greater unleasher in life than the very people you choose to run with. The people you run with will either lift you to new heights and pull you in their draft to greater success, or they will slow you down and hold you back to their pace or their level of achievement.

I have watched this phenomenon through the years as I have walked people through their journey of success. It is often very obvious as to who the right people are and who the wrong people are. A friend of mine was facing some very difficult personal challenges. He found himself picking up the pieces of poor decisions caused in part by the very people he was running with. It didn't take him very long to realize that he needed to find a new group of people to run with—people who would bring out his best, people who would call out greatness from the core of his being, people who would hold him to higher standards, people whose draft would carry him to true success.

The limitations you are being held by may very well be connected to the people who you have brought into your circle and who are influencing you. This is not to point the finger at them for where they are or their influence on you. What it does do, though, is point a finger at you. You are where you are by choices you have made along the way. It may be time for you to broaden the base of the people who speak into your life and leadership decisions.

This past weekend I had dinner with a gentleman from Pereira, Colombia. He has enjoyed great success in his professional and business pursuits and his future is looking as bright as ever. In our conversations about life, he asked me a probing question about marriage. My wife and I have been married for twenty-six years and are enjoying the blessing of our commitment to each other. His question came from his desire to experience the same. He simply asked about what it takes to make a marriage last. He had been married for ten years and he and his wife have a beautiful daughter. He wanted to know the key practices and strategies that would help him create and nurture a healthy, life-giving marriage.

YOU ARE WHERE YOU ARE BY CHOICES YOU HAVE MADE ALONG THE WAY.

This is exactly the reason why you want to make sure that you have the right people taking the journey with you, people who provide wisdom and perspective and have achieved levels of success that you hope to achieve as well. The right people will help you get to your preferred future faster. They will help you avoid common mistakes and missteps along the way. The right people are essential to breaking through your limitations so that you can achieve the success you want and live the life you deserve.

It has been said by a number of people that your network will determine your net worth. These are words of wisdom that cannot be ignored. When you hang with the right people they add value, they increase your net worth, and they increase the quality of your life and success pursuits. The right people call greatness out of you. Their pursuit of success inspires and fuels your pursuit of success. Their mindset forms and develops your mindset. Their personal and professional disciplines refine your personal and professional disciplines. As they unleash their leadership greatness, it empowers you to do the same for yourself.

THE RIGHT PEOPLE WILL HELP YOU GET TO YOUR PREFERRED FUTURE FASTER.

The right people lift you to new heights. They pull you in their draft. They help you get comfortable with revving your engine and going for greater success. There are three questions that you need to answer to implement and apply this chapter:

1. Who are the right people in my life right now?

_____

_____

_____

_____

_____

2. Who do I need to leave behind and move on?

_____

_____

_____

_____

_____

3. Who do I need to bring into my life and leadership that I can draft off of?

_____

_____

_____

_____

_____

Don't underestimate the power of the people you run with. They will determine your success trajectory and the time it takes for you to see your dreams come true.

THE POWER

I HAVE ALWAYS BEEN A raving fan of Marvel
Entertainment. They have brought to life super hu-
man characters like Spiderman, the Hulk, Captain
America, and my personal favorite, Iron Man.

I grew up watching a healthy dose of Superman,
Batman, Wonder Dog, and The Six Million Dollar
Man (aka the Bionic Man). These were my heroes, icons
and role models as a boy, which probably led me to the
thought that wouldn't it be cool if we had super powers?

What if we were able to leap tall buildings in a single bound, be more powerful than a locomotive, and go faster than a speeding bullet? Wouldn't it be cool if we could go beyond human limitations and do extraordinary things? What if we could somehow go beyond the limitations that hold us at low levels of achievement? If only. . .

YOU HAVE THE POWER TO GO BEYOND YOUR LIMITATIONS AND BARRIERS AND ACHIEVE EXTRAORDINARY RESULTS.

I want to help you see something that most people don't recognize; you actually do have superpowers. They are different than those of Superman or Captain America, but you possess your own set of superpowers.

You possess power and ability that I don't. You possess unique giftings and strengths that others don't have. You have a superpower encoding. Each of us was created with amazing and unique abilities that are part of our unique wiring.

One of the most satisfying things I do through my business, The Epic Advantage™, is to help people discover their superpower and then show them how to activate it and unleash it on the world. It is so rewarding and meaningful when I see someone realize their power and potential and then live a powerfully effective life.

A few days ago I sat with a client and talked through some of the challenges that she was facing in her field of work. She had an uncanny ability to create trust with clients fast. She was personable, engaging, calm, cool, collected, and a great conversationalist. She was comfortable and very competent in a sales role, and she excelled. She, by all accounts, was a rock-star performer.

YOU HAVE SUPERPOWER STRENGTHS!

The issue that she had to overcome is what I have seen as a very common struggle: we don't know to recognize our gifting for what it is, our superpower. Each one of us is encoded with special and unique abilities that make us who we are. The key to this truth is to make sure that we operate from our sweet spot of superpower and strength. When we operate in a manner consistent with our encoded abilities, we are able to leap tall buildings in a single bound.

On the other side of our strengths we find our weaknesses. The only thing that could limit the strength and potential of Superman was Kryptonite, a negative energy source that drained his strength and abilities. Everyone has deficiencies and far too many of us allow these weaknesses to dictate our life and limit our success. Instead of living from the strength of our wiring, we focus on our weaknesses and allow them to dumb us down and minimize our potential. Our weaknesses are our Kryptonite, and if we can identify them, we can steer clear of this power-draining source.

KNOW YOUR SUPERPOWER SO YOU CAN STAY AWAY FROM YOUR KRYPTONITE.

In my conversation and coaching with this client I took a few minutes to help her understand her superpowers. We use a tool that is the premiere performance and personality trait assessment in the world, Professional DynaMetric Programs or PDP®, to show people with precision accuracy who they are at the core of their being. PDP® helped me to see my strengths and abilities in a way that no other trait assessment had ever successfully done before, and it changed my life. Through PDP®, our personal profile reveals our superpowers. With the right insights you can know how to fully leverage what makes you awesome and how to unleash it on the world. You can, with precision accuracy, understand your areas of strength that can lead you to success and also the areas of weakness that will keep you from success.

I have walked hundreds of people through their own PDP® profile to help them understand their innate encoding, and the results are staggering. When people know what makes them unique, and they understand with precision what their strengths are, they can then lean fully into the best version of themselves. Most people don't know, especially with any degree of insight and accuracy, what makes them tick and what gives them the advantage in life and leadership, but you can. You have superpowers that when you are operating in them you will find more meaning, happiness, success, achievement, and joy.

There are two sides to our personal profile, the superpower side and the kryptonite side. The superpowers are our unique gifts and abilities. The kryptonite is the misuse, misunderstanding, or neglect of our unique abilities as well as our weaknesses.

I walked this young leader through the kryptonite of her profile that was limiting her success. While she was great with people and a very capable leader, her profile was also working against her. She allowed people to walk all over her. She allowed certain types of people to take advantage of her good will. She unknowingly demeaned herself, which influenced how others treated her and ultimately ran over her. Once she understood her unique profile and saw with precision accuracy her superpowers, she was able to confidently capitalize on these while simultaneously staying away from the kryptonite that was working against her and her success. It was a powerful moment when the lights came on; this truth changed her life. She went from an insecure and unsure person to Wonder Woman! She now knows her superpowers, and she leans into her strengths and abilities.

One of the challenges I see for professionals is that they do not have a clear and precise understanding of their strengths, abilities, and encoded advantages. Most people have a very general idea, but general ideas or solutions don't change the game for people and their performance or productivity. Others have a categorical idea in that they have used a personality profile to label them and provide categorical insight. Most personality profiles provide very general and very limiting categorical insights, which give a look at the surface but leave the depths of a person's true capacity and ability unrecognized.

With PDP® ProScan®, we help clients go far beyond generalizations and categorical information to provide precision performance insights. The results are mind blowingly spot on trending at 96% accuracy. The advantage that this depth of insight provides is a game changer. There are nine different focus points that ProScan® measures to provide the insight needed to understand a person's performance strengths and capacities. The only way to fully capture the power of PDP® ProScan® is to experience it yourself. Do what millions of others have done and let the precision insight of PDP® show you with 96% accuracy what your superpower abilities are and how you can live and lead from a place of strength, impact, meaning, and joy.

For more information, log onto TheEpicAdvantage.com and see how we are changing the world with Professional DynaMetric Programs (PDP®) for individuals, teams, and organizations. You can also reach out to us at ClientHelp@TheEpicAdvantage.com to request a ProScan® or to inquire about our team training and enterprise-system solutions for organizations and businesses.

YOU HAVE SUPERPOWERS. WHEN YOU ARE OPERATING IN THEM, YOU WILL FIND MORE MEANING, HAPPINESS, SUCCESS, ACHIEVEMENT, AND JOY.

Here are some questions for you to consider as you think through this chapter:

    1. What are your top three strengths (superpowers)?

_____

_____

_____

    2. What do you do well that seems effortless and fun?

_____

_____

_____

    3. What do other people say you are good at?

_____

_____

_____

    4. What do you love doing?

_____

_____

_____

5. Where do you shine?

_____

_____

_____

I want you to also think through your kryptonite:

1. What do others say you're not good at?

_____

_____

_____

2. What do you keep doing that feels awkward and unnatural?

_____

_____

_____

3. What do you suck at? (Yes, I said *suck!*)

_____

_____

_____

4. What doesn't come easily or naturally for you?

_____

_____

_____

5. What do you hate doing?

_____

_____

_____

Another form of kryptonite is the baggage that we unnecessarily carry through our lives. The baggage we carry is a significant limiter and leash that weighs us down and keeps us from living an extraordinary life. I vividly remember the day that I identified the baggage that I was carrying for most of my life and left it behind.

I met with a new client, and we walked through the results of their PDP® ProScan® report. The report is filled with profound insights regarding a person's performance traits and unique strengths which, when recognized, can increase their leadership intelligence and help them lead at higher altitudes of impact and effectiveness. Before we even opened the report, the executive

I was meeting with began to diminish and downgrade who she was as a person. She was the top performer for the company she was with, and yet all she could talk about was the negative side of who she was and how she performed.

LIVE FROM YOUR STRENGTH AND SUPERPOWER AND LEAVE YOUR SELF-DEFEATING BEHAVIORS BEHIND YOU.

As we walked through the profound insights of her report, it was very difficult for her to see the upside of her profile. Before I go any further, it's important to understand that our report focuses solely on a person's unique strengths and style. We help people with science-based data know with accuracy what makes them awesome and how they can leverage their "epicness" to accelerate opportunity and maximize performance.

Even though our report and assessment focuses on a person's strengths, the executive I was meeting with kept going back to what she felt was wrong with her. This was an obvious inhibitor, and a huge opportunity for me to help her let go of the baggage she had clearly been carrying around for a long time. I have been working in life and leadership development for over twenty-five years and what was obvious was that she had someone or perhaps several people in her life that demeaned and degraded who she was as a person. Over time, she accepted their assessment as truth and embraced their lies.

Perhaps someone had treated her harshly or berated her in her younger years. It is possible that someone heaped shame and blame on her that she continued to carry.

IT'S TIME TO SET THE BAGGAGE DOWN AND LEAVE IT WHERE IT LIES AND MOVE ON IN FREEDOM.

I can't speak to the source of the bad programming that had affected her, but what I can speak to is the self-defeating behaviors that weighed her down. She was well into life and carrying a heavy load of negative beliefs about herself and her value to the world. She was doing what I have done and what many people do. We carry unnecessary baggage on our journey of life. Unnecessary baggage is the result of unresolved issues, bad thinking, poor self-esteem, relational drama, unhealed hurts, internal conflict, mental and emotional wounds, and more.

I can tell you that this type of baggage will fatigue you like nothing else. It's time to set the baggage down and leave it where it lies and move on in freedom. The negative and destructive things people have spoken over your life in the past must be buried forever. The false truths about who you are as a person need to be silenced. The shame and blame that others heaped on you or that you heap on yourself must be discarded. To unleash greatness on the world, do yourself a favor and drop the baggage that has weighed you down and held you back and leap forward.

This is one of the elements of the work that I do through our executive coaching program that is so rewarding. I help people identify their baggage and then we help them leave it behind. And that's exactly what I hope you will do. There is a reason I feel it is so important to give our baggage a name; we need to know what we are dealing with and identify it with clarity and certainty. When you have clearly identified your baggage and attached a name to it, you are much quicker to recognize and call it out when it surfaces. It has not only been my observation but my experience as well that has taught me this valuable practice. When we leave things unchecked or we simply ignore them, they are quick to hide just below the surface and remain undetected by radar. Then, when we are least prepared, it pounces on us mercilessly and ambushes the greatness of our life.

Our personal baggage can affect us physically, mentally, emotionally, relationally, spiritually, and in many other ways. We were not designed to carry baggage for long periods of time. For some reason, we find it very difficult to let go of things that we have attached ourselves to even though they are destructive.

Do you know what your baggage is? Is it a dumb college decision that still haunts you? Is it your first, second, or third marriage that didn't work out? Is it getting unfairly fired from your dream job and your bitterness towards the person who fired you is consuming? Is it hatred for what someone did? Is it financial disaster that wrecked your life? Is it poor behavior that hurt others? Is it someone who wronged you and you can't let it go?

It is very important to know what your baggage is specifically. Like a Samsonite label on a suitcase, you need to label the baggage you have carried for too long so that you know what it is that is holding you back or slowing you down. There may be some pain that surfaces as you think through this, but allow yourself to courageously confront the baggage that is holding you back. There is no shame in acknowledging your baggage. Neither is there any honor in denying it.

When you begin to recognize your personal baggage, you then know how to travel forward much lighter and what baggage to leave behind. When you find yourself tempted to pick up the old baggage and resurrect the pain and problems of your past, you simply don't. You set it back down and you travel light. It is one of the most liberating moments when you finally set the baggage down for good and move on.

Take the time right now to identify and label your baggage:

1. What emotional baggage do you need to leave behind you?

   _____

   _____

   _____

2. What pain or past struggles do you need to move on from?

   _____

   _____

   _____

3. What negative things spoken over you in the past are you still allowing to limit the greatness of your life?

   _____

   _____

   _____

THE LEASH

I HAD JUST ARRIVED AT John Maxwell's home in West Palm Beach, Florida; I was star-struck and eager to learn from the master. For those of you who don't know who John is, he both literally and figuratively wrote the book on leadership. He is an international leadership coach who has invested his life in raising the tide of leadership globally. If you have ever read books on leadership, you've likely read a book or two of his.

We were gathered at his home that night for dinner, and it was one of those occasions where my eyes were wide open, and my mind was trying to absorb everything I possibly could. After introductions were made and conversations ensued, I found myself becoming more of an awe-struck spectator. Leadership engines were revving all around me, and they were large-bore engines. You could feel the rumble of the horsepower as leaders were doing what leaders do best. I watched and listened and marveled.

The best way to describe how I felt in that setting was like being at Churchill Downs at the Kentucky Derby as champion thoroughbreds thundered around the track; I felt as if I was being pulled into their gravitational draft, but I could not match their speed or strength.

TO UNLEASH YOUR GREATNESS, YOU MUST DEVELOP A GREATNESS MINDSET.

These tremendous leaders had clearly discovered the secrets of unleashing greatness, something that I would begin to discover as a direct result of my time with them. What I discovered that night was that to unleash greatness I had to develop a greatness mindset. Greatness unleashed first begins with great thinking.

Greatness is a mindset before it translates into action. I know in my case, I dreamed of achieving greatness. I had visions of greatness and success, but what was missing was the right mindset. I wanted it but didn't believe I could achieve it. I saw it in others, but I couldn't see it in myself.

My mind was not right, and clearly I was not living from a greatness mindset.

GET YOUR MIND RIGHT AND BE AMAZED AT WHAT YOU CAN ACCOMPLISH.

About this same time, a friend of mine who is a fitness trainer was helping me get my health and fitness headed in the right direction. I have to say he was an exceptional trainer, but he was brutal since his job was to whip me into shape.

I vividly recall a moment in the training where I was straining to complete the set he prescribed. My arms were trembling, my voice was whimpering, and I had my head bowed down in an effort to focus what strength I had left to finish the set. At that moment he asked me, "Where's your mind right now? Get your mind right! Where are you looking? Are you going down or going up?"

His voice of experience knew exactly what was taking place inside me. I was questioning whether I could complete the set, focusing on my weakness and perceived inability. My mind was definitely not right.

Instantly, when I heard his words, something snapped into place, "Look up and set your mind on success. Stop doubting, believe!" Low and behold, I found the strength to finish the set and go even further. Living with a greatness mindset is a key practice of living unleashed.

YOU MUST BELIEVE THAT GREATNESS IS YOUR DESTINY.

This was what I saw in that group of leaders at John Maxwell's house. They had a confidence and a sense of clarity that I was lacking. They had a success mindset, a greatness mindset. They believed greatness was their destiny, and they were unleashing their greatness on the world as a direct result of what they believed about their lives. This mindset is where I have observed many people struggle and even fail. I believe the limiting factor for most people is not their education or experience, nor opportunity, but their mindset. Their minds are not in the right place, and most allow fears, insecurities, inadequacies, and doubts to put a very low ceiling on their lives. To unleash greatness in your life, you will have to develop a disciplined, greatness mindset.

A GREATNESS MINDSET...

- Rejects thoughts of doubt and inadequacy.
- Refuses to allow fears and insecurities to limit expectation and taking action.
- Challenges your mind to take you to places you have never dreamed of before.
- Takes control of every thought and imagination and forces them to surrender to greatness.
- Believes that your dream can and will be achieved.

The greatness mindset involves embracing a few key thoughts to instruct and inspire you every day. Cultivating a greatness mindset is tough work in itself. Your mind will resist what you are trying to program it to think. It will fight you because it wants control. It will argue with you because it thinks it is right. But do not give in to your lesser self.

Unleash your greatness with great thoughts. When you take control of your thoughts and begin to focus on a greatness mindset, you will see things begin to change immediately. This has been the single greatest advantage I have discovered for my life: the greatness mindset is the first priority in unleashing your greatness on the world.

I was coaching a young professional who was a very promising, up-and-coming leader in the organization where he worked. This young man had developed the skills the job required and then some. There was every indication that he would go places and do great things. However, he began to create interpersonal roadblocks affecting his overall performance and life satisfaction.

We began to talk through his frustration and the drama that seemed to incessantly follow him. It became very clear that the primary issue he was struggling with was a mindset issue. He did not have an accurate nor healthy perspective on who he was and what he was capable of accomplishing. His mind was not in the right place and this was ambushing him.

THE QUESTION YOU HAVE TO ANSWER IS WHAT DO YOU BELIEVE ABOUT THE POTENTIAL OF YOUR LIFE?

As we uncovered the source of this poor mindset, we were able to then set in place greatness affirmations that he integrated into his life, and everyone took notice. He quickly found himself interacting much more positively with those around him and his relationship challenges began to fade away. He began to experience the power and advantage of a greatness mindset.

I want you to begin integrating the following "Greatness Mindset" exercises until you start seeing results. I am confident that once you see the results, you will want to keep doing these exercises. There is no magic formula to them, just simple mental investments you will make to get your mind right. Repeat after me:

- I was meant for a life of greatness.
- I have what it takes to achieve epic success.
- The best is yet to come.
- I reject thoughts of inadequacy, inferiority, and failure.
- I refuse to allow my fears, insecurities, and doubts to limit the greatness of my life.
- Today, I will unleash greatness on the world!

These simple statements hold the seeds of greatness that will produce fruit as you lean into your destiny. The question you have to answer is what do you believe about the potential of your life?

Take a few minutes to think through these questions:

1. What do I believe about the potential of my life?

_____

_____

_____

_____

_____

2. What thoughts do I need to change so that I can unleash greatness on the world?

_____

_____

_____

3. What thoughts are derailing my potential?

_____

_____

_____

4. What mindset is negatively affecting my performance and work and my contentment in life?

_____

_____

_____

5. What am I going to do to make positive mental investments in my life?

_____

_____

_____

It was the early 70's when my dad came home from work with a Golden Retriever puppy in his arms. I still remember my surprise as my dad handed me my first dog. Since it was the early seventies and my favorite cartoon to watch was none other than *Scooby Doo*, it took me about two seconds to give my new dog a name. You guessed it, Scooby Dooby Doo. In reality Scooby and I were both pups who would grow up together.

After a year or so Scooby was full grown, and he had far outpaced my growth. I remained a little boy while Scooby became a very large dog. One of Scooby's favorite activities was a walk down to the schoolyard just a block from our house. Like any young dog, Scooby would get all ramped up and ready to roll. On one particularly memorable walk, something down the street caught Scooby's attention, so much so that Scooby surged down the street at a pace that I could not control nor maintain.

I was a small boy, Scooby was a big dog, and I had more than my hands full of a situation that was about to go sideways, especially since I had naively tied the leash around my arm so that Scooby would not get away. Halfway down the street Scooby began to lunge forward, propelling me with him. I did everything a little boy could do to hold him back but to no avail. There was a section of the sidewalk that was covered with a thin layer of dirt, and when we hit that section, although my feet were planted, I continued to move forward, sliding on top of the dirt. At this point I was panicked; all I cared about was making sure that Scooby didn't get away.

As Scooby continued to pull and, as I continued to slide across the dirt-covered sidewalk, my feet hit an uneven uplift in the sidewalk. At this point the scene became even more comical, although painful. When I hit the trip hazard, my face went straight for the sidewalk, and I found myself being pulled in a prone position down the street as Scooby charged even harder.

After traveling several feet in this unfortunate position, Scooby finally slowed his excited surge, and I gained control and then composure. It was at that moment that I realized how strong Scooby was. Scooby had power and potential that I had leashed. I kept Scooby from fully displaying his ability; he was leashed to my limitations.

YOU HAVE AMAZING POWER AND POTENTIAL THAT MUST BE UNLEASHED!

I wish I could say that my experience that day with Scooby was the only time in my life that being leashed to something threw me down and drug me on the ground, but it isn't. In fact, I have found myself on several occasions being leashed to limitations, and these experiences were painfully brutal. In truth, we all have leashes that limit us: Leashes of our past. Leashes of our upbringing. Leashes of our mindset. Leashes of our pain. Leashes of the expectations of others. Leashes of circumstances or situations. Leashes of doubts. Fears. Insecurities.

WHAT LIMITATIONS ARE YOU LEASHED TO THAT MUST BE DOMINATED?

It is difficult to watch someone making the choice to allow their own leashes of limitations to go unnoticed and unchecked. I can tell you that I find it more than difficult watching a friend or co-worker, neighbor or family member allow themselves to be limited by their perceived limitations or inadequacies. And here's the deal, more often than not they choose the leash that holds them at very low levels of living and performance.

I want to repeat that statement so that you hear it and personalize it: When we are limited by leashes of limitations we must realize that the person who holds the leash is us. We are the ones who have wrapped those leashes so tightly around our wrists that we won't ever let them go.

I sat with a client the other day as she began to describe her current circumstance. She had the drill down like a script. She had rehearsed the excuses that have limited her for much of her life and have kept her at moderate success in her professional career. What was obvious to me was imperceptible to her; she chose the leashes that were limiting her potential, but she didn't recognize them. The leash that limited her was in her own hands. She had the power and ability to let go of it at any time, but instead she let herself be drug down the street so many times that it had become normal for her.

THE LEASH THAT HOLDS YOU AT LOW LEVELS OF PERFORMANCE AND RESULTS IS IN YOUR HANDS, SO UNLEASH YOURSELF.

As I listened to her story, I shared about my boyhood experiences with Scooby. I wanted her to see that she didn't have to tie herself to limitations, but that she had within her control the inner strength to let go of the leash, to completely cut herself free, and to let her true strength be known to the world. Her particular leash was her limiting beliefs about her worth, value, and personal power. She was raised in a home environment where she was controlled and dominated by other family members. She was never given permission to live the life she wanted to live and became subservient to the demands and dreams of others. She had become comfortable with being the doormat, and this fed into her adult life and relationships. She had the power to set herself free, but she accepted what she thought was her lot in life.

LET YOUR STRENGTH BE KNOWN TO THE WORLD.

As she sat across the table from me in a coaching session, I did everything I could to help her see her own worth and power. I called out the leash she was holding so tightly to, and helped her see that she is powerful and that her worth is far greater than she has ever known. It was a beautiful moment as she began to sit straight up in her chair with a confidence coming from a deep place. Her eyes sparkled and her voice was energized, as she recognized who she really is. Possibly for the first time in her life she was encouraged to see her personal value.

That is the gift I hope to give you as well. I want you to realize the true power and greatness of your life and that the leashes that you have been tethered to have no place in your pursuit of success. You have the power to cut those leashes and to leave them in the dust of your past.

We can put all of the right people around us and have all the support we need to succeed and live a meaningful life, but if we make the choice to hold the leash of limitations in our own hands, we will never fulfill the true greatness for which our lives were meant.

YOU HAVE THE INNER STRENGTH TO FINALLY LET GO OF THE LEASHES AND TO DRIVE YOUR LIFE FORWARD.

I know what it is like to have a grip so tight that our knuckles turn white for lack of blood flow. I know exactly what it is like to be tied to low levels of living and performance. I've been there, done that and have a few t-shirts to prove it. That was a part of my story, but it isn't any longer.

I want you to know that you can cut the leashes that limit, hinder, or hold you back, and you can live a bigger and better life. You have the inner strength to finally let go of all leashes and drive your life forward. Take a few minutes to answer the following questions:

1. What leashes have you held onto with an unrelenting grip?

_____

_____

_____

_____

2. What limiting lies have you accepted as your lot in life that must be corrected?

_____

_____

_____

_____

3. How are you allowing your thoughts or behaviors to limit the trajectory of your life?

_____

_____

_____

_____

_____

4. What choices have you made that have created limitations?

_____

_____

_____

_____

_____

5. What leash are you cutting yourself free from and leaving in the dust of your past?

_____

_____

_____

_____

_____

Let go of the leashes that are holding you back; leap forward and pursue epic!

THE WHALE SHARK

I HAVE STUDIED THE LIVES of more than a few people who would be labeled as rainmakers. A rainmaker is someone who creates excitement, energy, action, and traction. They are able to generate new clients, new accounts, new business, new opportunities, and new revenue streams. It seems as if they are able to make the impossible happen. To state the obvious, a rainmaker makes it rain.

I have been a student of success for all of my adult life, looking to find the secret or secrets that change the game. If a secret exists that can jettison my life and leadership to another dimension, I want to discover it.

After many years of searching and seeking, I came to a sobering and yet liberating conclusion: there are no real secrets to success. The Rainmakers that I learned from didn't have a special ancient formula for success. They didn't have secret magical powers that gave them superior abilities. They didn't have a magic potion that contradicted the natural world.

What I have learned and am learning, is that to be a rainmaker you have to make it rain. To unleash greatness, or accelerate opportunity, or maximize performance you must make it happen. In other words, the success you are looking for has no short cuts or secret formulas; it will only come as you act on your dreams and desires and MAKE THEM HAPPEN.

If there is a secret to success, it's this: success comes as a result of diligence, determination, and discipline. Success is a result of a little bit of luck, but it's mostly a result of hard work.

If you want to be a rainmaker, get ready for a little bit or, more likely, a lot of blood, sweat, and tears. Years ago when the organization I founded was hitting its peak of success, I had a few detractors out there who despised our growth and success. These antagonists would often make back-handed remarks and snippy statements in their efforts to justify why they were not seeing the success we were experiencing. The bottom line to our success then and now is that my team and I put in the work to make it rain.

THE SECRET OF SUCCESS IS THAT THERE IS NO SECRET; YOU MUST MAKE YOUR SUCCESS HAPPEN.

I don't believe for a minute that I am a natural-born rainmaker or that I have dialed in the secret formula that guarantees success. To be honest, I fail frequently, and I hate it, but it is part of what it takes to win.

Success is the result of diligent, determined, and disciplined work, and a lot of it. I cannot state this fact strongly enough, but for you to maximize your performance and unleash greatness on the world, you must be willing to make the steep climb on an arduous route.

There have been many times when I have wanted to slow down or step back or even bow out all for one reason—the path to success is extremely demanding. If you haven't already, you will likely find yourself consumed with thoughts that your journey is too hard, taking too long, requiring too much of you to be worth it. Let me tell you, your success is on the other side of a long, steep, painful climb. I know that's not very motivational of me to say this to you, but it's the truth.

SUCCESS IS A RESULT OF A LITTLE BIT OF LUCK, BUT IT'S MOSTLY A RESULT OF HARD WORK.

I invited the wisdom of an executive leader to help me navigate some next steps as I led my organization forward as well as to help me see the success I desired to attain personally. In our conversations I was eager and ready for his coaching and insight. With eager anticipation I listened to every word. He made a statement that has stuck with me, "Jerome, to get from where you are now to where you want to be will be determined by the level of pain you are willing to endure."

My hidden response was, "Wait, what?" I cannot say that his words excited or inspired me, not in the least in fact, but I knew what he said was right and true. The path to success requires an inner strength to endure the demands and pain of the pursuit of greatness. There is no easy way around this; greatness requires great effort. Greatness requires great suffering. Greatness requires great work.

The question at the root of the pursuit of greatness is simply this, "How bad do you want it?" Do you want it bad enough to make the necessary sacrifices? Do you want it bad enough to take the risks associated with success? Do you want it bad enough to pay the price, regardless of what that price is? Do you want it bad enough to endure the pain, the pressures, and the problems of greatness?

GREATNESS REQUIRES GREAT WORK, GREAT PAIN, GREAT EFFORT, GREAT ENDURANCE.

I have watched far too many people walk away from their dreams because the price was too great or the pain was too much. I have found myself at times balking at the fast pitch of success. I've been in a leadership role for over twenty-five years, twenty of which were executive-level roles. I have yet to find a time in my success journey that didn't require sacrifice, deep determination, and an uncomfortable amount of discipline. The secret sauce of rainmakers is that there is no secret sauce. Rainmakers pay the price, and they endure the demands of their dreams. Rainmaking is not easy, it is not for the faint of heart, and it is definitely the road less traveled. But if you stay its course, you will find success. I have to wonder how many dreams have been left or abandoned due to the price required to see them fulfilled. Our world creates very soft people who want success to come easy and when it takes longer, or requires more, or the pain gets to intense, people bail. If we could only see what could have been if someone would have paid the price and put in the work.

Your journey will be no exception. You will face adversity. Your dreams will require discomfort. You will become a close friend to pain. You will be forced to endure difficulty. But know this, you are equal to the task and the fulfillment of your dreams and the achievement of your success is THROUGH, not around, your pain.

YOU'VE GOT WHAT IT TAKES TO ENDURE THE PAIN AND ACHIEVE YOUR DREAMS.

We were headed out for an afternoon snorkeling excursion off the Belize Barrier Reef when our tour guide received word that a whale shark had been spotted in the area. To make the opportunity even more exciting, the guide shared with us that whale sharks don't typically enter the interior of the barrier reef, especially in January, so this was a big deal even to the Belizeans. I had on my bucket list to someday swim with the gentle, graceful, and giant whale sharks. They are behemoths in the chain of marine-life mammals, and they welcome the company of people from time to time. These creatures are the picture of poetry in motion as they skim the surface of the water with their mouths wide open, capturing the tiny plankton and then descending into the deep, dark-blue depths of the ocean. There is also a menacing component to them, though, and it's not just their size. They have a dorsal fin and tail like a massive shark. In fact, at first glance you take a second look to make sure that it's not a man-eating shark.

SUCCESS WILL NOT WAIT FOR YOU; YOU MUST BE READY FOR IT.

As we left the dock in our triple-engine boat, the captain hit the throttle, and we made our way to the last known location of the whale shark. Our guide began to prep us with insights that had relevance not just to the immediate moment but to life as well. As the boat raced across the interior of the barrier reef, the guide shouted instructions, "The whale shark will not wait for you; you've got to be ready. Get your gear on because when we come up on him you have to jump in and swim. The whale shark will not wait for you!"

His point was well taken and well made. In short, when opportunity knocks, you need to be ready in advance to take action. So we furiously put our fins on as well as prepped our masks and snorkels to take the plunge if and when the moment arrived. We all sat anxiously awaiting the moment; we listened to our guide, and we were ready. The signal came from the boat captain that a whale shark was just ahead. It was like a scene from *The Fast and the Furious*, as each of us scrambled to a place of advantage to capture every ounce of opportunity we were being given. "One hundred feet! Eighty feet! Get ready! Fifty feet! JUMP! SWIM!" If there had been a way to capture that moment on video, I am certain we would all get a good laugh out of it as we jumped or were pushed overboard, some of us in front of the graceful beast and some of us right on top of it. Wow, it was a rush! Although we had been instructed not to touch the whale shark, I not only ran my hands down the length of his body, I grabbed hold of his dorsal fin and enjoyed the ride, as he began to descend into the depths. It was a magical moment. As we climbed back into the boat, we were all jubilant and boisterous. The only descriptor powerful enough to describe the unbelievable experience was of course EPIC.

PREPARATION IS NEVER WASTED.

What we had experienced was in part due to luck but also due to being prepared. If we had ignored the guide's instructions to be ready, we would have missed the experience of actually swimming with the whale shark and would have had to settle for watching from a distance. Luck is a part of success. Every now and then you show up at the right time and the right place, as we did that day in Belize. However, luck has a way of favoring the prepared. I have observed that success is more about being prepared for it and less about "Lady Luck" showing up. It has never ceased to amaze me that the more prepared I am, the more luck I have. In reality, luck is only a small part of the success journey. The reality is the more prepared you are, the more opportunity you will create.

I recently watched an episode of *Running Wild* with Bear Grylls as he was in the middle of tackling one of nature's obstacle courses. To get where he wanted to go he had to cross a river with several feet of snow on each bank. The water temperature was freezing and the air temperature was below freezing. Before he stripped down to cross the river, he packed his backpack with tree bark so that as soon as he arrived on the other side, he would be prepared to start a fire and save his life before hypothermia took its toll. As Bear stuffed his pack with the last bit of bark and tender for the fire, he made a profound statement, "Preparation is rarely wasted." When he got to the other side he was ready to save his own life. He didn't wait to get there to prepare, he prepared before his life was in danger. That insight alone is a strategic difference from those who achieve epic success and those who don't. You cannot sit around waiting for success to show up; you must prepare for it, and be ready when it shows up. In the words of Bear Grylls, "Preparation is rarely wasted."

THE MORE PREPARED YOU ARE, THE MORE OPPORTUNITY YOU WILL CREATE.

What many people consider luck, chance, or gratuitous opportunity, I often see as the result of hard work, action, and preparedness. Don't get me wrong, every now and then I have simply been lucky, but I was ready for it when it came. When you are ready, you maximize performance and accelerate opportunity. I wish I could say that I was ready for each moment when luck showed up, but that wouldn't be true. I have missed my fair share of opportunities that I still kick myself for. The missed opportunities have not been wasted; I use them as fuel to kick my butt into gear and prepare for luck to show up again.

Preparation followed by action is the name of the game to maximize your performance. Whatever it is that you want and are pursuing, you must prepare. You must master the art of preparedness and do the work before "luck" shows up. When you do the hard work of preparing, you shine like a rock star when opportunity presents itself. You will blow the minds of friends, clients, and your competition when you stay ahead of the game by being diligent and disciplined in getting ready for success. The very thing keeping you from the life and success you want may be your lack of preparation. There's no way to predict what's coming and what life is going to throw at you or bring to you, but you must prepare yourself for what could be. Preparation sets the stage for success to show up and for "Lady Luck" to shine on you.

This past weekend I competed in the Master of the Mountain Quadrathlon in Raton, New Mexico. This is a fun race, as it involves an intense, six-mile mountain run, a three-mile mountain lake kayak, a twenty-mile biking leg, and a shotgun target and trap shoot for the finish. When we arrived for the race orientation meeting the night before, the event coordinators ran through the specifics of the race. As they walked through the stages and routes, there were a couple of things that caught me by surprise: most importantly, the bike leg was going to be nearly twice the length that I thought it would be. This would have some complexities for me, as I was only prepared with enough hydration for what I thought the race was going to be. But this is where my training and preparation were going to come into play, since I had been training for the unexpected. For months I trained with limited hydration as well as diverse terrain and circumstances. I would ride for up to two hours of intense riding with very limited water intake. The point was to condition my body for the unexpected. What my training prepared me for was to go farther on less and endure the demand. Thankfully, I was prepared.

There is a long line of people who were not ready when opportunity knocked, and I have been in that line once or twice myself. People standing in the line of missed opportunity talk about what could have been and what should have been. In fact, many spend so much time lamenting over missed opportunity that they waste even more time and often miss the next opportunity that surfaces. If that's where you are, get out of that line and get in the whale shark line. Be ready for her when she comes, because she won't wait for you.

To personalize this chapter, carefully think through the following questions:

1. What preparations do you need to make to create your success?

_____

_____

_____

_____

_____

2. What areas of your pursuits need some development so that when opportunity knocks you can rock and roll?

_____

_____

_____

_____

3. In what ways are you not ready for success?

_____

_____

_____

_____

_____

4. What are you going to do every day to prepare for the success you want and deserve?

_____

_____

_____

_____

How you are going to accelerate your performance
and maximize your opportunities?

_____

_____

_____

_____

_____

_____

EPIC-LOGUE

AUTHOR **STEVEN PRESSFIELD WROTE** in his bestselling book, *The War of Art*, that "the enemy of creativity is resistance." Pressfield calls out the many manifestations of resistance and what he describes so perfectly is that the things keeping you from the fulfillment of your dreams and desires do not come from extrinsic factors, like the economy or opportunity, but rather from a lack of intrinsic resolve, such as grit, self-discipline, and determination.

I have read and listened to *The War of Art* more times than I can count, and here's why: it helps me identify the real inhibitors to my dreams. The single greatest battle that wars against our success is that we ignore the real reasons why our dreams are not manifesting; we are not fighting a fierce enough battle. There is a dragon that must be slain, and that dragon is resistance. You are the ONLY knight who can slay it.

YOU MUST SLAY THE DRAGON OF RESISTANCE AND FIGHT A FIERCE BATTLE FOR YOUR SUCCESS.

When I was twenty-three years old I shared with one of my sisters that I would be a published author by the time I was twenty-five. I was well-intentioned but frankly young and dumb. I had the talent and the capacity to write, but I was not aware of this menacing dragon that would be relentlessly unmerciful. I was clueless that the fulfillment of my dreams required an ongoing battle against self-defeating behaviors. I had not learned the art of dragon-slaying.

To help you understand the fierceness of the dragon of self-defeating behaviors, I want you to enter the story of *The Hobbit* written by J.R.R. Tolkien. Tolkien created a menacing and fierce dragon that destroyed everything in its path. Smaug was its name and it showed no mercy. Smaug was the defender of the riches of Erebor, which was formerly the dwarf kingdom. Smaug was a fierce force to be reckoned with, and to war against him would not be for the timid or weak, but for the bold and strong. With valiant effort and audacious courage, the dwarves warred against Smaug in an effort to regain what rightfully belonged to them, the riches and kingdom of Erebor. They engaged in an epic battle to take possession of their dream, and if you want your dreams to come true, you must do the same.

AN EXTRAORDINARY LIFE OF GREATNESS IS NOT FOR THE TIMID OR WEAK, BUT FOR THE BOLD AND STRONG.

If you are now picturing that the dragon you must slay is a fire-breathing monstrosity and that it ruthlessly and tirelessly works to destroy your potential, you are finally getting a glimpse of what I am talking about. It's time for your own "Desolation of Smaug" epic thriller, and it's time for you to slay your dragon. The dragon of resistance is a formidable adversary that tirelessly works to keep you from success or achievement. The dragon of resistance is committed to its cause, to dumb you down and imprison you in a life of mediocrity. Resistance revels in its ability to keep dreams and desires from ever becoming reality.

Even as I pursue my personal dreams and aspirations today, I must unsheathe my dragon-slaying sword, and slay resistance every single day. If I choose to ignore the resolve of the dragon of resistance, I will have set myself up for mediocrity and normalcy. Your success is waiting at the end of your sword. Unsheathe your sword and slay your dragons. Whatever it is that is keeping you from unleashing your greatness—slay it. Whatever it is that is stopping you from accelerating opportunity—slay it. Whatever it is that is keeping you from maximizing your performance—slay it. Take out your sword, defend your kingdom, and slay your dragons!

UNSHEATHE YOUR DRAGON-SLAYING SWORD, AND SLAY RESISTANCE EVERY SINGLE DAY.

The art of dragon-slaying is perfected in the daily practice of taking personal responsibility for the outcome of your life. The greatest dragon-slayers are not those who abdicate their fight to someone or something else, but those who firmly hold sword in hand and who stand strong against the tactics of resistance. Let me challenge you to call out the dragon of resistance that is keeping you from writing your book, starting your business, pursuing your dreams, inventing the solution, discovering the cure, unleashing your greatness. Call it out. Don't let it keep you living in the land of the lazy or living a life that is lame. Only you can slay your dragon!

Your success and achievement can be released when you unsheathe your sword and slay your dragons every day. The battle against resistance is a never-ending one that requires your tenacity and diligence, but it is a battle you can win. If we could somehow replay the tape of human history and see all of the ideas, solutions, inventions, cures, creations, and dreams that fell prey to resistance, what would we see? Imagine for a moment just the possibilities that never became a reality in the last 100 years. There is a graveyard of "what if," "if only," and "what could have been." This is a sad reality for far too many people and dreams. But this doesn't have to be your story; you can do something about it. You can slay the dragon and valiantly pursue the successful achievement of your dreams and desires.

While there is a vast graveyard of dreams that will never be realized, there is also a world filled with people who have defeated the dragon of resistance and who saw their hopes and dreams fulfilled. Look at the developments just in our young country since its inception. We are an industrious and action-oriented people who do the hard work of dragon-slaying and who see our dreams fulfilled. No success comes without taking the sword in hand and slaying our dragons of resistance. I want you to take a sober moment of reflection to think through ways that the dragon of resistance is working against you:

1. How are you giving in to resistance?

_____

_____

_____

_____

_____

_____

2. How are you allowing resistance to slow you down or stop you completely?

_____

_____

_____

_____

_____

3. What do you need to give diligent attention to?

_____

_____

_____

_____

4. What do you need to finish?

_____

_____

_____

_____

_____

5. What do you need to start?

_____

_____

_____

_____

_____

6. What do you need to make happen that you've been struggling to do?

_____

_____

_____

_____

_____

You are your own knight in shining armor. It's time to unsheathe your sword and slay your dragons.

YOUR SUCCESS IS GOING TO COME DOWN TO ONE THING, THE CHOICES YOU MAKE EVERY DAY.

The final step in this book is the most difficult step of all: what are you going to do with what you've read? Your success is going to come down to one thing, the choices you make every day. Your next step involves speed of implementation and massive action. The quicker you apply what you've read, the faster you will move in the direction of your dreams. The faster you implement the ideas that I have presented, the quicker you will see the results that change the game.

Let me ask you to think through what you've read. What is your #1 takeaway from this book? It may be hard to narrow this down to just one, and if this is the case, write down the takeaways that you want to influence you as you lead forward. Once you've written your list of one or more, select the number-one, game-changing insight and then do everything in your power to focus on conquering it. Implement the #1 takeaway immediately and keep doing it until it becomes second nature.

WHAT IS YOUR #1 TAKEAWAY FROM THIS BOOK?

_____

_____

_____

_____

_____

_____

Your success and personal significance are in your hands. It's your responsibility to unleash greatness, accelerate opportunity, and maximize performance. No one can do it for you. This is up to you and it's on you. Keep this in focus: your results are proportionate to the action you take, so take massive action fast! The pages of this book are filled with the epic advantages that you need for success and living a life of significance. Read them and reread them until you resolve to bring the change that you committed to in the introduction of this book.

I will leave you with words of wisdom that come from an early 1800's Shawnee leader, Chief Tecumseh, "Live your life that the fear of death can never enter your heart. Love your life, perfect your life, beautify all things in your life. Seek to make your life long and of service to people. Prepare a noble death song for the day when you go over the great divide. Always give a word or sign of salute when meeting or passing a friend, or even a stranger, if in a lonely place. Show respect to all people, but grovel to none. When you rise in the morning, give thanks for the light, for your life, for your strength. Give thanks for your food and for the joy of living. If you see no reason to give thanks, the fault lies in yourself. Abuse no one and no thing, for abuse turns the wise ones to fools and robs the spirit of its vision. When your time comes to die, be not like those whose hearts are filled with fear of death, so that when their time comes they weep and pray for a little more time to live their lives over again in a different way. Sing your death song, and die like a hero going home."

This is your mission, and should you accept it, your extraordinary life starts now. LIVE UNLEASHED!

ABOUT JEROME WADE

 Jerome Wade is an author, international speaker, executive coach, global adventurer, and the Chief Epic Officer of The Epic Advantage™. Jerome is passionate about helping people live an extraordinary life by unleashing their greatness on the world. As an entrepreneur, he has successfully launched and led two not-for-profit organizations and two for-profit businesses.

YOU CAN CONNECT WITH JEROME AT:

- Twitter.com/JeromeWade
- Facebook.com/Jerome.Wade
- LinkedIn.com/in/JeromeWade
- www.TheEpicAdvantage.com
- USA 505.463.7234
- Jerome@TheEpicAdvantage.com

PROFESSIONAL SPEAKING INFORMATION

To book Jerome to speak for your event or organization, please contact BookJerome@TheEpicAdvantage.com. For more information on Jerome's professional speaking programs log onto www.TheEpicAdvantage.com.

THE EPIC ADVANTAGE™

UNLEASH GREATNESS

THE EPIC ADVANTAGE™ SOLUTIONS

The Epic Advantage™ works with growth minded business professionals who want to SELECT, DEVELOP, and RETAIN top performers.

Our solutions include precision performance assessments, conference and event speaking, corporate workshops and training programs, team development seminars, organizational culture and leadership development, and PDP® Integrated Management Systems.

To discover how we can specifically help you lead your people, team, or organization forward please give us a call at 505.463.7234 or reach out to us via email at ClientHelp@TheEpicAdvantage.com or you can log onto TheEpicAdvantage.com.

PDP® PRECISION PERFORMANCE ASSESSMENTS

For more information about PDP® ProScan®, Team-Scan®, and JobScan®, precision performance assessments, please log onto TheEpicAdvantage.com. You can request a DEMO today to personally experience the power and precision of PDP®.

If you are interested in becoming a retailer or distributor of PDP® to expand your current coaching and consulting business or you want to launch a new business please call us today!

Made in the USA
San Bernardino, CA
23 December 2016